3D Materials and Construction Possibilities

PEG ROBINSON

Cavendish
Square

New York

Published in 2018 by Cavendish Square Publishing, LLC
243 5th Avenue, Suite 136, New York, NY 10016

Website: cavendishsq.com

This publication represents the opinions and views of the author based on his or her personal experience, knowledge, and research. The information in this book serves as a general guide only. The author and publisher have used their best efforts in preparing this book and disclaim liability rising directly or indirectly from the use and application of this book.

All websites were available and accurate when this book was sent to press.

Library of Congress Cataloging-in-Publication Data

Names: Robinson, Peg.
Title: 3D materials and construction possibilities / Peg Robinson.
Description: New York : Cavendish Square Publishing, 2018. | Series: Project learning with 3D printing | Includes bibliographical references and index.
Identifiers: ISBN 9781502634238 (pbk.) |
ISBN 9781502631466 (library bound) | ISBN 9781502631473 (ebook)
Subjects: LCSH: Three-dimensional printing--Juvenile literature.
Classification: LCC TS171.95 R63 2018 | DDC 621.9/88--dc23

Editorial Director: David McNamara
Editor: Fletcher Doyle
Copy Editor: Nathan Heidelberger
Associate Art Director: Amy Greenan
Designer: Alan Sliwinski
Production Coordinator: Karol Szymczuk
Photo Research: J8 Media

Printed in the United States of America

CONTENTS

On the cover: Reinforced concrete was used to print this two-story villa in Beijing. It was the first home printed on-site and not printed in pieces elsewhere and assembled.

TECHNICAL TERMS

extrude To squeeze a material out. For example, a pasta machine extrudes pasta dough.

microwelding Joining metals using heat; welding on a very small scale.

scaffold A 3D-printed structure designed to provide support for further 3D printing: a frame or skeleton that carries less rigid layers of printed material.

sintering Joining layers of a 3D printing material using heat or laser.

CHAPTER ONE

Expanding Uses

THIS IS A BOOK FOCUSING ON THE MATERIALS USED IN 3D printing. The topic will be the kinds of printing already in common use, and others that are likely to become more common in the future. The book will also evaluate how 3D technology will change the job market, from construction to medicine, in the years to come.

We are living in a time of enormous change. Manufacturing systems are growing and shifting today as much as they did during the Industrial Revolution of the 1700s–1800s. Back then, there were changes in where people could find work and what kind of work people would be hired to do. That changed the kinds of training

Opposite: People can create many products using 3D printing, including this lacy stiletto shoe.

they needed. People who'd been educated for farmwork or to serve as craftsmen often ended up starving and homeless on the roads of Europe. Few were prepared for the new labor markets of the time. Many were forced into jobs as domestic workers or in factories. Those who learned the technology of the times, though, were lucky. They became mechanics, engineers, machinists, and

Students can learn to engineer parts for cars and other moving objects using 3D printing tools and materials.

machine operators, and they enjoyed prosperity unlike any they had known before.

Similar patterns are happening in the United States today. People are fighting to adjust to the changes technology brings. The problem is not always that there are fewer jobs. Instead, there are *different* jobs. To be employed in the future, you will need to prepare yourself for the jobs of the future.

What kinds of jobs will need 3D printing skills? Many. Maybe even most. There are few areas of production that won't have some contact at some level with 3D printing in the future. Right now, 3D technology is changing engineering, automotive technology, toy manufacture, medicine, computer engineering, space exploration, building and construction, cooking, and more. We are employing 3D tech on the smallest possible scale, with nanotech, to products the size of human building projects—homes, apartment complexes, and more. That's where this book comes in—discussing the many materials used in 3D, and the possible ways materials may be used in the years to come.

The History of 3D Printing

3D printing is a new technology developed only a few decades ago. But 3D printing can also be thought of as ancient—or at least as old as printing itself. We call 3D printing **additive manufacturing (AM)** because it is cumulative. That means it builds things by adding layers to create many effects. Old-fashioned, ink-based printing was the very start of cumulative printing–adding layers. It only added one thin, thin layer, though. Even when layering many colors of ink to get illustrations, the whole idea of old-style printing was to stay in one flat, thin dimension. It is still important to remember, though, that printing has always been about adding layers. It took cleverness to think of stacking the layers higher and printing with heavier materials than thin ink. At the same period, more and more work was being done with **noninvasive imaging systems** in medicine and other sciences, taking apart 3D shapes into layer after layer, which could then be restacked on computers or using light tables. The idea of layering was commonplace and always of interest during that period.

If it was not a major leap of genius, it was a giant leap in terms of how we can create things. The idea of using layering to print a complicated shape immediately opened doors to producing objects it would be very difficult to make any other way, just as noninvasive imaging allowed doctors and other scientists to explore things that could otherwise only be seen using destructive techniques.

The first group of people to run with this idea worked in design engineering. They imagined printing out layers of a design using plastic to create prototype models of their projects. At that time, creating mock-ups was painstaking, demanded superb craftsmen, and was costly. With complicated objects, there were difficulties fully describing the shape for the crafters. However, there was already access to sliced, layered images using **computer-aided design (CAD)** software; if you designed your project in CAD, the computer could easily determine what each layer looked like. If all you were worried about was the shape, you ought to be able to print out the layers and get a prototype.

Needless to say, it worked brilliantly.

The Dawn of 3D Printing: Plastic Prototypes

The first material chosen for 3D printing was plastic. It was an obvious choice in many ways. It could be solid or fluid. It could already be sprayed and **extruded**. It was inexpensive, held complex shapes, and wasn't very fragile. Taken all together, it is no surprise that it was the first choice for 3D printing experimentation. It remains the most common material used in 3D printing, though other choices are rapidly gaining acceptance.

In 1984, two patents were filed for stereolithic (3D) printers. The first was filed by French designers Alain Le Méhauté, Olivier de Witte, and Jean-Claude André. Their patent application was abandoned, however, as their company saw no business application for the new technology. This left room for the second patent, filed three weeks later by American designer Chuck Hull of 3D Systems Corporation. Two years later, the patent was granted. Hull's design is generally accounted as the first official 3D printer. Hull's machine used several strategies commonly used at the time: laying down photopolymers (light-reactive plastics) and curing them (bonding and solidifying them) with ultraviolet light. Hull's primary contribution to the whole design was in software design rather than physical design. He improved on the software used to describe shapes to the printer, producing an even and elegant result.

Software was one of many problems facing early developers. No matter what you want to make with a 3D printer, you must be able to communicate how it is to be done to the printer in a clear fashion. If you are printing in plastics, the printer has to heat and extrude the printing material. That material has to be able to stick to the previous layer below, and to the next layer above. If you are printing with resins, or metals, ceramics, and similar materials, this is done by applying heat or light to the material—which is often in a powder form—to create a bond. This process is commonly called **sintering**. The software controls the heat or light source.

Sintering

There are three common methods of sintering most manufacturing materials: **fused deposition modeling (FDM)**, **stereolithography (SL or SLA)**, and **selective laser sintering (SLS)**. Of these methods, FDM and SLA are commonly found in both commercial

Direct metal laser sintering machines are built to shield us from their powerful lasers.

and hobby printing. They are comparatively safe and controllable techniques, most commonly used for plastics and resins. The laser technology used in SLS is both more expensive and more dangerous, and is less commonly found outside of high-tech manufacturing.

Each method has its advantages and its disadvantages, and each is commonly used with particular materials. The most common materials used for FDM printing are plastics. Computer software is used to define the shape and placement of a layer of the final product. This is called **slicing**, and the program is called a slicer. Once the shape is determined, a thin thread of plastic is passed through a heated cone, which heats the plastic to just barely its **melting point** and feeds it out like icing from a cake-decorating tool. The feed lays down a layer in the correct shape, just hot enough to squeeze out and bond to the earlier layers.

Resin is the material most commonly used for SLA 3D printing. Resins are liquid plastics that are hardened using ultraviolet (UV) light. The printing method is very different from FDM production. FDM lays down layers of melted plastic in the same way ink flows out of a fountain pen, or caulk from a caulking gun. SLA printing uses a holding tank of liquid resin, and precise ultraviolet lasers to cure the resin layer by layer and create a finished product.

The third common method of sintering, called SLS or **direct metal laser sintering (DMLS)**, is most commonly used with metals, both in large-scale and small-scale uses. Using this method, powdered metal is laid down by the printer. Then a very precise, hot laser is used to heat the powder to just barely melting—hot enough to bond, not hot enough to flow. This is called **microwelding**.

These three methods cover the most common methods and materials used in 3D printing. They are not the only methods or materials, but they are among the first methods and materials used, and they are widespread and available to many people and organizations.

All these methods of printing involve adding layers of material, stacking them up like pancakes or layers of bricks. They add material, starting from nothing and building up, rather than starting with a big block of something and cutting down. Because they add material, they're collectively called AM, or additive manufacturing.

Bioprinting

Bioprinting is a broad term for an even broader array of methods and technologies. At its very broadest, the word can include the use of scientific analysis to develop and modify models of three-dimensional artifacts for use in daily life, including basic tools and architecture. More commonly, though, the term is used to indicate a variety of ways of modeling, printing, and synthesizing biological models and artificial organs. Work is under way for bioprinting to support the production of fully functioning transplantable organs and body parts, though that technology is still in its infancy.

The most common use of bioprinting is in the creation of extremely accurate and realistic models

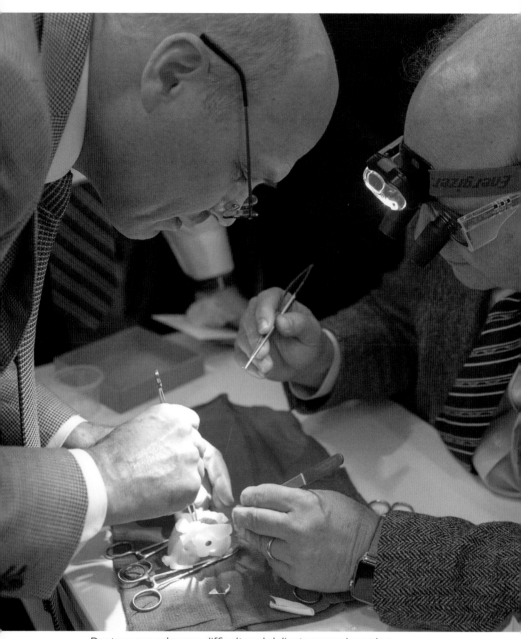

Doctors can rehearse difficult and delicate surgeries using 3D-printed organs made from scans of a patient.

of parts of the body. These parts must be as realistic as possible because they are used in research of many types. Many pharmaceutical companies welcome the ability to test medicines on nearly perfect models of human organs, for example. These models, made using biological materials, are not useful for transplant purposes, but they can inform researchers of likely problems with various applications.

Similarly, models of this kind can be used by doctors to plan and rehearse complicated surgical procedures. A range of bioprinting and biomodeling methods have been used to plan heart and brain surgeries, to determine how best to separate conjoined twins, and to practice these plans ahead of time. This sort of planning and practice means that even extremely challenging, long surgeries requiring large surgical teams can be done using teams familiar with every stage of the surgery.

This is important because every human is medically unique. We all share a lot in common, but we are as varied inside our bodies as our faces, our voices, and our fingerprints are varied. Our illnesses, injuries, and defects are also unique. No two tumors are identical. No two sets of conjoined twins have been joined in the same way. No reconstruction of damage from an injury is exactly like another. Most of the time that does not matter. In complicated cases, though, a doctor's knowledge of the unique problems can make the difference between life and death.

Bioprinting first uses the many medical noninvasive techniques of imaging what's inside our bodies to create a computer model. **Computed tomography (CT)** and magnetic resonance imaging (MRI) are two of the common methods used to develop a three-dimensional image of a medical condition. Biopsy, too, may be used to ensure accuracy all the way down to a cellular level. Then a variety of materials may be used to build a model based on the computer analysis. The resulting model can be used with high levels of trust when practicing the treatment that will follow. Medical teams can go in well rehearsed and ready for what awaits them.

There is also hope that bioprinting will, in time, allow the production of fully transplantable human organs. Progress is already being made in producing artificial skin, using a **biodegradable scaffold**—an artificial material used to support layers of normal human skin cells. The results of this research are not yet in common use. Doctors, however, have great hope that this type of artificial skin will save the lives of people suffering massive burns and other injuries.

A quick consideration of the many forms of bioprinting, and the differing goals of the field, shows that there are many materials and techniques that can be used. A researcher who wants a model for testing has different needs than a doctor planning a complicated surgery or trying to save a burn victim.

Bioprinting uses multiple types of printer, too, to deal with the many materials used. Some have two print heads: one to lay down cells, and one to lay down a scaffold material to support the cells. Some are similar to ink-jet printers, using cartridges to hold **bioinks**. Others work using six-axis systems that allow the computer to print the muscles of a heart separately from the veins, making production more efficient.

Aerospace and Aviation

Aerospace and aviation have become major areas using 3D printing technology. The techniques involved in printing metals, especially using DMLS and SLS, have allowed NASA and private aerospace and aviation companies to manufacture complex parts quickly and efficiently. The quality of the products is very high. As a result, designers can push the boundaries of technology further. They know the technology is there that will let them try new things or do old things better.

The 3D printing technology is of particular interest to aerospace designers because it allows the manufacture of materials in space, without gravity to take into account. There are many reasons these are important to think about. The first is safety. The old methods of casting or forging metal or kilning ceramics are dangerous in space. A fire on a space station would be hard to contain and would use precious oxygen, contaminating the ventilation systems and damaging the interior of the spacecraft. The danger of fires and explosions rules out traditional techniques. Traditional manufacturing also depends on gravity to contribute to the process of

THREE SCALES OF PRINTER

There are now three different scales of 3D printing. Each is adapted to different goals and types of product. There is a common scale that produces objects or parts of objects that are generally small enough to be handled and manipulated by ordinary people. Printers

In the future, printed apartment buildings like this one in China will be more common.

of this scale create the objects that fill our lives: cups and plates, prostheses and medical implants, jewelry and sports equipment.

Second, there are printers that work on a much smaller scale. These microprinters use resins and lasers to create microscopic products. They create electronics gear, computer components, nanotechnology for medical programs, and similar items. This class of printer is vital to support a kingdom of technology powerful far beyond its size—a kingdom of technologies that can change how we think about our world.

The third group goes the other way, from human scale to titanic creations. The same plotting and additive approach used in ordinary 3D printing is now being applied to construction and similar "big job" problems. These huge printers are already being used in construction and are expected to become common on a geological scale, with landscaping and terraforming projects that will change how we address agriculture, conservation, and recreation.

These three scales of 3D printing have developed over little more than a decade. There is every reason to expect that even more styles and scales of printer will be designed.

things like casting—or must replace gravity with pressure injection systems. The old methods also convert metals to complete liquids, which can behave oddly when gravity is not present. Think of videos you've seen of astronauts playing with liquid blobs on the space station. Then think of blobs of melted, hot steel!

The advantage of 3D printing in space is that it is safe, easily controlled, and produces highest-quality products. It will allow astronauts to make tools and products for their own use in space, but it also opens up the possibility of developing factories in space. Many of the asteroids in space are rich in metals and chemicals. Imagine being able to mine the asteroids, process the ore in space, then manufacture products to ship back to Earth!

The Future of 3D Printing

The techniques of 3D printing are very new, and the possibilities extend far beyond the progress most people experience. New boundaries are being broken even now, and the techniques are being used in many new ways. Can you imagine how 3D printing might be used in restaurants and food factories? People are already exploring that possibility. What about construction? Yes: not every building is put up with hammer and nails. In China, a six-story apartment building was printed in 2015. There are plans under way in Dubai, United Arab Emirates, to build a skyscraper with huge, construction-scaled 3D printing rigs using concrete compounds as their ink. The techniques are used in jewelry making, and to manufacture high-tech auto parts. Artists are creating delicate ceramic sculptures using 3D printers. People have printed out an entire working car, with all elements created using 3D printers and materials. The possibilities keep growing. Imagine having a problem with your car, and instead of being told that the part isn't in stock and has to be ordered, the garage simply prints out a new one. It is a real possibility.

In the future, there will be few people who do not have any contact with 3D printers and printed objects. The ability to use these materials and machines will be a useful skill to offer employers, or even to use for daily life. From professional uses to home uses, 3D printers are likely to become as normal and necessary as ordinary printers already are. That will mean learning the STEM skills that go with the technology: math skills, the ability to use computer-aided design software, the knowledge to use the software that develops layers for printers to print out, or the more complicated software that decides how to build interlocking structures independently, rather than as crosscut layers.

Every age has necessary skills that even beginners need. In our day and age, it is hard to get any job without reading, writing, mathematics, and computer skills. In the years to come, those requirements are going to only become more intense, with a special focus on science- and math-related skills. Preparing for that time is a smart move that will make it easier to learn to use 3D printers.

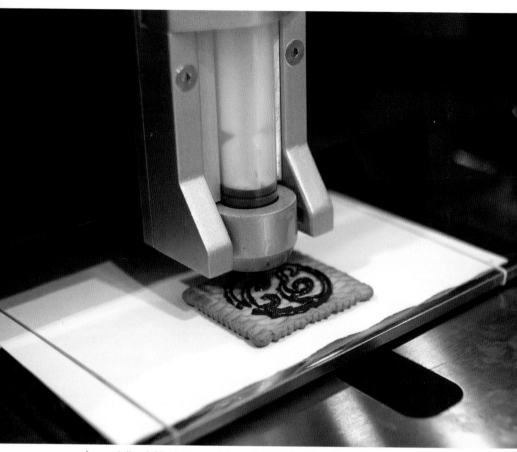

A specialized 3D device prints out the icing detail on a cookie and can help with the decoration of other baked items.

Jobs in the Future

For much of the twentieth century, people could expect to get jobs at all levels of education and to keep those jobs for their entire lives. Only a small number of people needed to worry about careful planning to make sure they were employable, or retraining for new positions.

This is no longer the case. There are fewer and fewer jobs for those with limited education, and even those with college educations need to plan carefully and get training that is likely to be useful in as many fields as possible.

More and more of the jobs that are expected to become available in the future demand strong training in science and mathematics—the STEM skills. They are foundational skills that support later training in related career skills. Some career skills are expected to prove widely useful.

Experts in the prediction of developing job markets expect 3D printing to create a wide range of new jobs and to be connected with a number of jobs that never before needed that technology. Once, for example, a factory worker might have needed at least some training as a machinist. That has become less and less true as manufacturing methods have changed. In the future, it is likely that the same workers will need some training in the science behind 3D printing and in the way 3D printers work. Once, office workers didn't even need to know how to use a typewriter. They counted on a secretarial pool to do their typing. Now, typing is done using word processing programs on computers. Everyone needs to be able to type and to understand how to use the computers we rely on.

3D printing is expected to have a very similar effect. It is likely to become so common that it impacts almost all jobs and demands that most people have at least some understanding of the technology involved. That includes having some math and science skills to use the machines effectively.

Job fields that are likely to involve some degree of familiarity with 3D printers include almost all forms of dentistry; surgery and any form of medicine that involves implants and prostheses; prosthetic design; engineering; manufacturing at all levels, from research and development to factory-floor creation and assembly; food production; jewelry design; educational jobs; prop making and applying makeup for stage and films; novelty design and manufacture; computer and electronics design and manufacture; almost all forms of commercial design; automotive maintenance; art production of all types, including sculpture and work in three-dimensional media; weapons design and manufacture; sports equipment design and manufacture; and household management. The list could go on. Just as computers eventually ended up affecting everyone in thousands of ways, 3D printing is likely to be part of most people's lives.

Improved Products

Why? Because like computers, 3D printers have such an enormous range of things they can offer us. These printers not only offer a newer, better way to make the same old things, but in many cases they allow us to make newer, better products. The method of production encourages the design of better products in the first place. The method also provides products with fewer flaws generated by the system of manufacture. All manufacturing methods create flaws as they proceed. However, the better the system, the fewer the flaws; 3D printing reduces the number of flaws.

As a result, almost any job involved in any kind of creation of physical objects is going to involve some kind of skill with 3D printing, just as any work that involved communication and data management ended up involving computers. Creation and manufacture won't be limited to 3D printing, but it is going to become one of the main methods.

That means that people planning their education need to look to a future filled with 3D printers and employers who expect their workers to use those printers. The smart planners will make sure they've got training in STEM skills. They will learn to use CAD software. They will study the materials used in 3D printing. They will set themselves up for future success.

TECHNICAL TERMS

petrochemical   Chemicals derived from fossil fuels such as petroleum.

thermoplastic   A plastic that can be repeatedly melted and formed into new shapes.

thermoset plastic   A plastic that can be melted and formed into a shape only once and never again.

CHAPTER TWO

Plastics

PLASTICS ARE THE MOST COMMON MATERIALS USED IN 3D printing. Plastics, also known as polymers, are a family of materials made of many repeating chemical units. They come in two major categories: **thermoset**, and **thermoplastic**. Thermoset plastics can be heated and shaped once. At this time they set solid, and they can't be melted and shaped again. Thermoplastic polymers, however, can be melted and reshaped an infinite number of times, and they can be recycled time after time into new products. The plastics used in 3D printing are thermoplastic polymers. They can be shaped once into a convenient form for a printer—most

Opposite: Filaments used in 3D printing come in many colors and in different kinds of plastics.

often into either **filaments** or into spherical beads. Then the printer can use heat or light to sinter the material, melting it and laying it down to form a new shape.

This is a very convenient way to make things. Thermoplastic materials allow designers to recycle their waste. This allows our culture to collect and reuse plastics, keeping our environment clean and making thrifty, sensible use of our resources. Plastics are a good choice for many purposes, and we use them in all walks of life. There is no career in America that does not deal with some form of plastic, in some manner, every day. Even low-tech jobs, or ancient arts and crafts, find uses for plastics: as packaging, storage, protection, and more.

Many Types

There are many kinds of plastics in daily use. Some are biodegradable. Some are not. Some are soft and flexible. Others are as rigid as metal or wood. Some work well in medical settings. Others, like latex, can trigger allergic responses and are dangerous in some medical uses. Many plastics are used in 3D printing. However, there are three main plastics in 3D printing: **acrylonitrile butadiene styrene (ABS)**, **polylactic acid (PLA)**, and nylon. Other plastics are available for printing but are less common. Every plastic has its own traits or characteristics. These characteristics all have an effect on which plastic a designer will choose for a project. Everything, including cost, melting temperature, strength and durability, and chemical composition, can change a designer's choice. Understanding the nature of each plastic will make it easier to decide what plastic you would prefer to use for your own projects.

ABS

Acrylonitrile butadiene styrene (ABS) may be the most popular plastic used in 3D printing. It is easy to understand what kind of plastic it is: Legos are made of ABS. It is used in many of the same ways PVC is used—as plumbing pipes, for example. It is a sturdy, rigid plastic that takes a high shine. It doesn't break easily. When it does, it shatters, like rock. It is hard enough to take a sharp edge. It is durable, somewhat heat resistant, and cheap. It can be glued easily and sanded cleanly. It is a good, stable, long-lived plastic that comes in many colors. It is suited to most projects needing a rigid, stable plastic.

It is a petrochemical-based plastic, meaning it is made of oil-related resources, and it gets its name from its chemical structure. Like many petrochemicals, when heated it gives off fumes. As such, you may require special ventilating equipment to work with ABS safely, including high-tech fans and filters in work labs, or hoods and masks to protect workers from the fumes. ABS may require a special printer with its own built-in HEPA filter. (HEPA filters remove particles from the air; they are designed to capture 99.97 percent of airborne particles.)

Like many other petrochemical-based products, ABS is not biodegradable. While it can be recycled, if it is just thrown away it will not break down and "return to nature." A child's toy made of ABS can be lost and buried, only to be dug up decades later almost unchanged. It will not rust; it is unlikely to stain. Its colors may fade in sunlight, but the actual plastic will not alter. It does not attract moisture as much as nylon, but it is **hydroscopic** (tending to absorb water through the air) enough to demand that ABS filament be carefully stored and kept away from humidity.

Applications

ABS is popular because it is suited to a wide range of applications and projects. It is stable, rigid, and resistant to pressure, heat, and shock. It can take a lot of abuse. It is easy to shape and easy to glue to other materials or to more ABS plastic.

In professional settings, the material is used for items such as kitchen implements, garden tools, storage containers, and bases to support further design and construction. It is useful for casings and for small-device control switches, dials, and handles. It can warp during printing but is less likely to do so in small pieces than in larger pieces. When using it, it is best to try to keep projects small or to design a project as multiple pieces that are later assembled.

It is suited for long-term projects intended to resist damage in many situations. It is water resistant, resistant to heat and cold, and to wear and tear. It can be used indoors and outdoors.

It is worth some concern in student projects because of the problem of fumes. Unless schools have access to the kind of ventilation, safety equipment, and specialized enclosed printers used to protect workers, it might be wiser to choose other materials. That said, with the correct ventilation and safety devices, ABS plastic would be a great choice for many designs.

PLA

Polylactic acid (PLA) is the second most commonly used plastic for printing, coming in after ABS. It is a hard, rigid plastic. It is slightly brittle. When used in ways that expose it to pressure, designers must plan for the stress. Like ABS and nylon, it is produced as a filament that can be guided through a **hot end** that melts and directs the plastic where it belongs, slowly building a complex object.

Among the most important facts you should know about PLA is that it is biodegradable. Given time and exposure to the right elements, it will break down and disappear, returning to the environment as a safe part of the soil. This makes it a perfect choice for a wide range of items that are supposed to be temporary. In medicine, PLA is used to support healing. It will eventually dissolve without the doctors needing to take any further action. In manufacturing, it can be used to provide disposable objects that will last long enough to serve their

PLA plastic can be recycled and is food safe, making it a great choice for disposable packaging and utensils.

owners, then be taken back into the ecosystem without doing damage.

For students, that means the ability to produce a prototype or learn the skills of 3D printing without leaving beginners' projects behind if they are not wanted: you can throw your practice runs away. Students will also appreciate that it smells comparatively good and does not expose them to fumes from oil-based plastics.

PLA is made of biomass. That means it is made from natural resources found in plants. These resources include sugars, starches, and cellulose. Most plastics are not made from biomass but from petrochemicals of one type or another. Many plastics are not biodegradable at all, or are very, very slow to break down. Some are considered serious ecological problems, lasting millions of years and endangering entire environments. PLA presents none of these problems. It is a healthy choice for the planet and equally healthy for human medical use.

PLA is also inexpensive. Because it is made of biomass, it is a low-cost plastic to produce, and the savings is passed on to the customers. This makes it a common choice for anyone planning a product that does not have to be stable and safe from decay and structural collapse, which can include food-service items, hygiene products, plastic wrapping and packaging products, and other throwaway items.

It is comparatively easy to create with. It should be carefully stored, as the plastic filament, like the finished product, is biodegradable. You do not need a heated **print bed** to make it work, though some people recommend one regardless. The material can be modified with sanding, painting, and similar treatments. However, it does not glue as well as some other plastics. The plastic itself is safe and breaks down into the environment without danger or complications. However, you should check to determine if colors used in PLA are similarly safe. Be aware that when PLA is exposed to natural conditions of water, sunlight, and microbes, it will break down. When intentionally placed in the environment or in a human body, it usually breaks down in between six months to a year.

Applications

As stated, PLA is particularly popular in the medical field and for bioprinting. PLA provides implants, biodegradable scaffolding for other forms of bioprinting, screws and plates intended to strengthen surgical mends, and similar items. Whether used in a pure state or serving as a support and structure for other biomaterials, including bioinks, it is a vital part of a growing medical reliance on 3D printing.

This has led to a growing industry focusing on the use of PLA 3D printing to manufacture medical implantable hardware of all sorts. The field of medical manufacturing is as varied as the industries that produce hardware or automotive parts. The companies involved are making the "nails and screws" of medical repair. The men and women designing these objects need strong STEM educations, both in computer-assisted design and engineering, and in medicine. They need to be able to imagine new items a doctor or surgeon would find useful. That takes at least some medical background. Then they need to be able to design a product that will be inexpensive to produce, perform to a high standard, be easy to manufacture, and take advantage of the materials used. Sometimes teams, working together, can spread out the necessary knowledge among their members, but

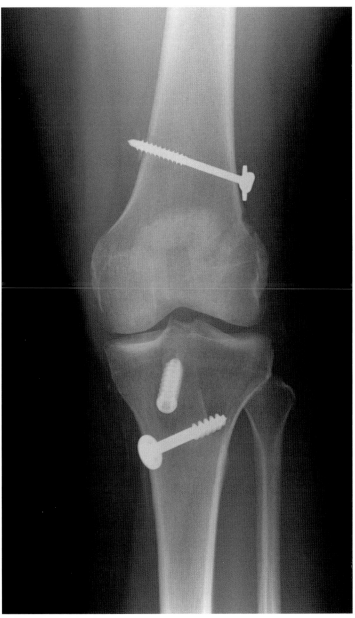

In one of many medical applications, plastic screws and pins help stabilize broken bones.

STUDENT DESIGNS A PROSTHESIS

It is exciting to see all the things 3D printing can accomplish. It can be difficult, though, to imagine how you might design and execute a project using that technology. What would you make? Why? How would you decide how to make your product?

It can help to see how other people have used 3D printers to do practical things. By seeing what they did and how they did it, you can understand the process better.

Oluseun Taiwo, a student at Northern Illinois University, recently decided he wanted to make a prosthetic hand that would help Sarah Valentiner play the violin. Valentiner, a middle-school student in DeKalb, Illinois, was born without a right hand. She already had a prosthetic hand that allowed her to bow her violin. It had been provided by the local Shriners. It was heavy, though, and difficult to use. A better prosthesis would make playing easier and more fun. Her parents, hoping someone could help, had signed up with an online group called e-Nable, which connects people who need prosthetics to volunteers around the globe with prosthetic design skills. They also checked with Northern Illinois University's College of Engineering and Engineering Technology to try to find someone who would be interested in helping Sarah.

Federico Sciammarella, an associate professor of engineering at NIU specializing in 3D printing, had a student he thought would be interested in the challenge. He contacted Taiwo, who was excited by the design challenge the project offered. He and Valentiner reviewed the situation. They talked through all the things that were involved and what Valentiner thought she needed. Taiwo had to decide how the prosthesis would attach to her arm and how it would hold the bow. It had to be easier to use than Valentiner's original bowing prosthesis. They decided it could be lighter. It had to be stable enough to let Valentiner apply steady pressure on the bow, or the pitch of the notes would change.

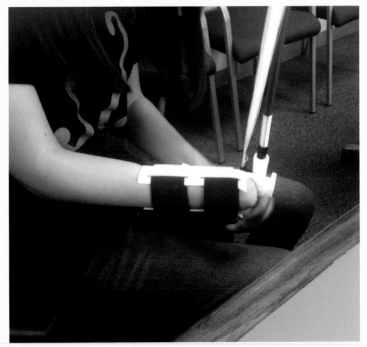

Sarah Valentiner wears her new bowing prosthetic, which was designed with Oluseun Taiwo.

When you work on projects like this, the first thing you must do is decide what is needed. Then you work through what can give you that result. Valentiner and Taiwo succeeded in making a lighter, stronger prosthesis that gave Valentiner more confidence in her bowing. It took them six drafts before they had a finished product that both felt was right. After each draft, they evaluated the project and asked what they could do better. Each time they found new ways to improve their work.

Any project you undertake using 3D printing offers room for that kind of process. Because 3D printing is fast and often inexpensive, it is possible to try and try again. The cost is low and the rewards are great when you can print out a draft of your design, test it, evaluate it, and then go back to the design to make it better. The combination of strong design skills and convenient printing encourage creative solutions to difficult problems. Even students can change lives by using 3D printing and good design techniques.

the more designers know themselves, the better they can serve their team.

More STEM education is needed in other areas of medical design using PLA in 3D. In these areas, researchers and doctors are using 3D printers, PLA, and a range of biomaterials to create model organs for use in research and education. They are working to create artificial organs that can be transplanted into people. They are also creating starter organs that act almost like seeds and soil, to grow new parts for people that can develop both inside the body and out. While this work can eventually develop into an industry, it is more likely to remain a small-scale industry focusing on biological objects tailored to each patient. The advantage of using PLA as a base for this sort of work is that it is medically nonintrusive, and when a real medical organ is grown, the supporting PLA dissolves and is gone.

Most PLA design and production requires some STEM training, but not as much as bioprinting. Designers developing packaging materials still need to understand some engineering and computer-assisted design, and they must be good at the math needed to determine efficient production systems. They do not, however, have to be research scientists. This area provides a lot of room for students who want to learn the basics of 3D printing techniques early. They can work with the machines and the filaments, learn how to use CAD systems, and discover how to take full advantage of the possibilities offered by the material.

PLA is a good choice for student projects. It is designed to be safe, stable, and wholesome. It is strong, rigid enough to provide a stable base for further additions, and inexpensive. A school with a CAD lab and access to a PLA printer and filament can give students a great chance to do the same kind of work they could end up doing professionally, and to experience the kind of information they need to do the job well.

Nylon

Nylon is one of the oldest synthetic materials. It was developed in the 1930s by DuPont and has been used widely for a variety of purposes ever since. A plastic, nylon is durable. Depending on how it is used, it can be very rigid or very flexible. Because nylon is so adaptable, it is a popular choice in 3D printing projects, though not as common as PLA and ABS. Nylon is often called "polyamide" when used in 3D printing. "Nylon" is the common term for a group of plastics. "Polyamide" is the term for the chemical structure of nylon. In 3D printing, though, "nylon" usually refers to filament nylon. "Polyamide" usually refers to nylon in a powdered form, sintered by tightly aimed lasers.

The nylon used for 3D printing comes as a thin thread, or filament, as do several other forms of plastic. The filaments come in many colors. The filament is fed through a guide attached to a moving head that traces out each layer of the 3D project. The nylon is heated to

240 degrees Celsius (464 degrees Fahrenheit), which is its melting temperature. The mechanism that guides and melts the nylon is called the hot end. The melted nylon is then extruded–pushed out like toothpaste–and laid down along a traced track plotted by the computer.

Nylon is hydroscopic. Even the spools of filament attract moisture, becoming damp from water vapor in the air. Manufacturers must choose between drying the filament before using it or printing it when wet.

Lasers sculpted material into these parts, which were then removed from the powder bed and cleaned.

PICKING
A PLASTIC

How do you choose a plastic to use for a 3D printing project? Several things have to be taken into account.

First, you need to know what kinds of plastic and plastic filaments your printer or printers can handle.

After you've determined the limits of your printer, consider the nature of your project. Does it need to be rigid? Flexible? Do you want it to last forever? Do you want it to be biodegradable? Which of the available plastics works best for this kind of project? Read reviews and evaluations of the plastics that you are considering.

Calculate the amount of material you will need to complete your project. Check costs. There are online sites that offer information for calculating the cost of printing jobs. Some are 3D printing services and will be including service fees. Others offer pricing spreadsheets to make it easier to calculate your expected cost.

If you can, test the materials. If you are working with a large lab, you may be able to test materials they have in stock. You may need to purchase your own samples. Run a test with a sample to see if you like the result.

If you do not have access to a printer or to a print lab, you may want to hire an online print service to produce your project. It will cut into the experience you gain in managing the machine and the process, but you will still get the experience of designing your project and preparing the design for printing.

Dry filament prints out a smooth, glossy product with a sleek surface. Moist filament prints out a bubbled, pitted product with a rough surface. The nylon can be dried over a period of six to eight hours at 71°C–82°C (160°F–180°F).

The powdered form of nylon, polyamide, requires a very different printing process. The spherical grains of powder spread out evenly, allowing designers to create even layers of consistent density and thickness. Each new layer is spread, then sintered to the whole using the heat of lasers, at a temperature of 170°C (338°F). This kind of printing takes place on a flat print bed in a tank. The grains are laid down with an arm that feeds the material onto the bed. The lasers then sinter the material, following the track determined by the splitter program.

Applications

Nylon has both benefits and drawbacks. It is not very heat resistant and melts at lower temperatures than most plastics, though PLA is similarly heat sensitive. The bond between layers is comparatively weak. It has good impact resistance. That means it takes bumps and drops fairly well, with little damage or breakage. Nylon is considered strong and durable, though, as well as being flexible, and is considered a good choice for a wide range of applications. It is often used in manufacturing for small machine parts, tools, plastic objects such as gaming pieces, and other items that demand some strength and

This cleaned and assembled nylon wrench was printed in a powder bed.

durability, but not the sort of strength offered by metals or high-tech ceramics. You can find printed nylon cogs and gears for small mechanical items, interior fittings for computers and laptops, and toys. The primary concerns are the level of strength and durability needed. Wind-up toys and laptops are not likely to need the strength or durability of titanium, so they are likely to be made with nylon.

The material is waterproof, resists corrosion, and is tough, flexible, and light. It is not very rigid. It is a low-friction material, which can be useful when you need parts to slide easily but less useful when you need them to resist motion. Nylon parts bend under pressure. If the pressure is going to be light, this may be no problem–gears and cogs and moving parts turning with light pressure will hold their shapes and work well. Increase the strain and the parts will bend and flex, failing to transfer force properly.

These suggest that nylon is useful in both high-tech, highly precise uses, and in far more informal and low-tech applications. The material serves well for 3D models–the original use of 3D printing. It is also useful in any application that does not demand extreme levels of rigidity and durability.

Nylon and polyamide powder are also both popular in medical printing. They are **biocompatible**, do not set off allergic/immune responses, and are light and strong, with just enough flex to serve well in many applications. The material is often used for prostheses, forming the main portion of a prosthesis or serving as a supporting player with other materials. Nylon printed materials can also serve as implants, replacing missing bone and cartilage, valves, and many other body parts.

Nylon projects for schools might include designing small hand tools, cases for mobile phones, small robots, experimental mobile remote-control units, game parts, the interior and exterior of wind-up toys, jewelry, sculptures, and similar small objects. Polyamide can be similarly used, with greater flexibility in precision work and complex sculpting. Both can be used to develop and design practical prostheses, and classes have actually developed prostheses for other young people in need.

Less Common Plastics

The three materials discussed above are the most common plastics in 3D printing right now. There are many other plastics in use, though.

- Vinyl is the same plastic used in old upholstery, flooring, and records. It is not in common use, but there are filament spools available. It is very fussy about its melting temperature but is considered to be less likely to warp than many other plastics. People have used 3D printers to reproduce classic vinyl records.
- **High-impact polystyrene (HIPS)** is similar to ABS. It is hard and, as its name suggests, it resists sharp impact. It takes up ink and paint well, and is easily decorated. It is easily joined to other pieces of HIPS plastic using limonene as a solvent in the same way PVC is joined using solvent.
- **Thermoplastic elastomer (TPE)** is noteworthy because it can be printed into a soft, stretchy product. While so many plastics used in 3D printing are rigid to some degree, TPE is flexible and elastic.

Still more plastics are under development, and it is always worth checking to determine what possibilities are available for projects and which printers can be used in printing with them. However, the primary three–ABS, PLA, and nylon/polyamide–are the most likely to be used for nonindustrial projects.

Wrapping Up Plastics

Plastics are currently the main material used in printing. They are most accessible to students and hobbyists just learning to use 3D technology. They offer reliable characteristics that make it possible to choose the best material for the best job. There are other plastics in use in 3D printing, but they play a comparatively minor role. Less commonplace plastics, like vinyl, high-impact polystyrene (HIPS), and thermoplastic elastomer, have their own traits, characteristics, and uses, but are seldom available to students in 3D printing labs.

They are, however, available to manufacturers around the country, and more will become available over the next few decades. The practical uses of 3D printing in manufacturing have become clear, and the ability to use every possible material appropriately is going to drive even more development.

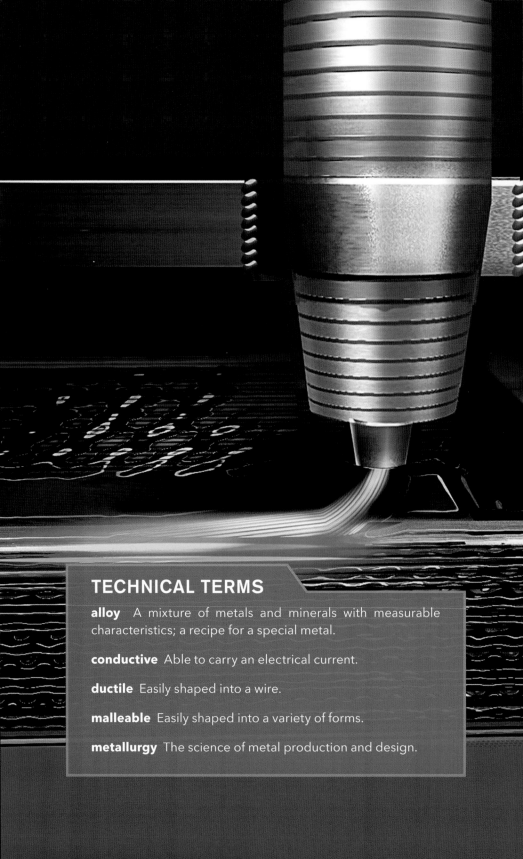

TECHNICAL TERMS

alloy A mixture of metals and minerals with measurable characteristics; a recipe for a special metal.

conductive Able to carry an electrical current.

ductile Easily shaped into a wire.

malleable Easily shaped into a variety of forms.

metallurgy The science of metal production and design.

CHAPTER THREE

Metals

PLASTICS ARE THE COMMON MAN'S MATERIAL FOR 3D printing. Almost anyone can get access to a 3D plastics printer. The materials are inexpensive, and the machines that use them are affordable and generally quite safe. The products can range from hard, durable, lasting objects to disposable items intended to be used once and thrown in the trash, soon to become biodegradable compost. If you limited your scope to plastics, you might never realize what a powerful technology has been developed in 3D printing.

Metals take you into the world of high-performance automobiles, of airplanes and space stations. Metals

Opposite: A metallic ribbon is extruded through the hot end. Printers of this kind are rapidly being developed.

bring you to the 3D printer as a powerful tool for manufacturing on a global scale, and possibly even beyond. It is metals that start people dreaming of factories in orbit around distant planets, of mining the metal of the asteroids. 3D printing gives designers access to technology ready to deal with complicated, difficult shapes and challenging metals—a technology ready to do things that were sometimes impossible to do to the same standard using old methods. The resulting pieces are as strong as those produced by older methods. The metal products of 3D printing do not have the problems caused by the old casting system. They do not have the lines left by casting, nor do they need the kind of cleanup that cast parts often do.

Metals also invite you to the world of **microprinting** and **nanoprinting**, which is printing on the smallest scale. The technology is used to create computer parts and microtools. Constructed with the delicate touch of laser light, metal products of 3D printing can be incredibly tiny and incredibly precise. These 3D printing techniques allow the construction of complex laces of resins and metals that can be measured in microns (1 micron is equivalent to 0.001 millimeters, or 0.000039 inches). They are microscopically detailed devices small as a grain of sand.

It is in metal manufacture that SLS printing comes into its own. This is the same method of printing described in the previous chapter when discussing polyamide printing—only in this case the beads that form

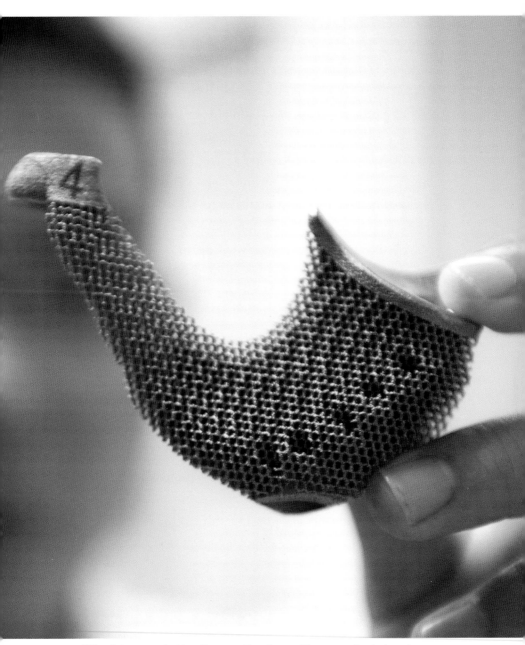

3D printers are better than casting for making complicated and delicate objects, such as this replacement vertebra.

the layers on the print bed are powdered metal, and the sintering is done using very high heat lasers. This method of printing doesn't squeeze out a molten toothpaste line of material to bond onto the previous layer. Instead, it guides a precisely targeted beam of light to quickly bond new powder onto old. No physical tool has to touch the new layer after it has been spread over the one before. Light alone touches the new material. Extremely hot and precisely aimed, the laser heats the metal powder to the melting point in a flash, and then moves on.

The SLS system is in many ways an improvement on old casting methods. There are no seams. There is little need to clean up the finished object. There are few flaws in the finished product. There are fewer bubbles, weak points, or cracks. SLS allows creators to develop highly complex shapes that would have been expensive or even impossible to manufacture using previous techniques.

Metals, particularly copper, are just beginning to make their way into amateur and general-access 3D printing. This is seen particularly in wearable electronic jewelry but can be used in a range of ways for other projects, too.

Metal objects produced using 3D printing methods do not come out of the printer bright and shiny. However, metals produced by forging or casting are also seldom bright. The glossy, reflective surface we are used to associating with metal is the result of a polishing process. Objects made with a 3D printer can be polished in the same way as other metal objects.

Steel

Steel was the metal that ushered in the industrial age. Improvements in creating steel alloys, and manufacturing objects with those alloys, led to hundreds of new commercial products available to both individuals and to corporations. The quality of steel and the ease of production opened doors to economic growth and provided work for thousands at all levels of society. Skyscrapers were made possible by the strength of steel.

New technology opens doors in our time, too, but our new jobs are often available to knowledge workers. These

The Light Rider, from Airbus APWorks, is the world's first 3D-printed motorcycle.

jobs demand skilled labor and education. The work in 3D printing of steel products illustrates this situation.

Making products with 3D printing is a form of manufacture. It requires many designers with STEM educations who can use CAD software and who understand the chemistry and engineering involved in **metallurgy**. There are also jobs for people who can use the 3D printing machines. These workers would oversee production and make sure the printer works properly and is maintained. This type of position requires education similar to that of a capable engineer or machinist. This presents our culture with a challenge. We must provide skilled workers who can offer that level of skilled labor. However, we also get to enjoy the products 3D printing can create.

Steel is one of the most common materials used in manufacture related to the aerospace and aviation industries. It is also used in prototyping and manufacturing parts for other high-performance fields, from race-car design to high-speed public rail.

Most of the 3D printing done with steel and other metals is done using a powder bed and selective laser melting (SLM), SLS, or DMLS printing techniques based on laser sintering. A third common family of techniques is called metal deposition (MD). This comes in two fundamental forms. The first is called directed energy deposition (DED), or laser cladding (LC). In DED printing, a robot arm places powdered material and microwelds it using a laser. This avoids the need for a powder bed. The second technique, used almost entirely for large-scale manufacturing in the military-industrial market, is called electron beam additive manufacturing (EBAM). This technique is a form of filament-based 3D printing. A robot arm carries a thin wire of titanium and fuses it in small, solder-like dots to build a much larger structure.

Industrial manufacture using 3D printing includes many optimized machine parts. These have been developed to use metal with great efficiency. The process allows designers to calculate how much metal any portion of a machine part needs to be strong, and what parts can function well with less metal. The end result is a part that is often lighter, stronger, and less likely to fail, and that needs less metal, allowing savings in materials. The finished products are often improvements on the original designs.

These techniques are not generally accessible to the average person. The methods are so expensive and specialized that they are almost entirely limited to industrial use. Methods exist, however, to create simulated metal prints. Most of these use some form of filament printing with an embedded metallic coloring agent. The resulting printing looks as though it were printed from metal, when it is really printed from plastic.

Applications

Steel is an alloy of iron. Alloys are combinations of different metals and minerals, each one with its own strengths and weaknesses. There are hundreds of recipes for different kinds of steel–there are even many different recipes for stainless steel, which resists rust. Each recipe produces steel with its own characteristics. These traits are not changed by 3D printing. This means that applications for 3D printing of steel will depend on what alloys are used, and what strengths and weaknesses are available. Stainless steels do not rust and can be used in situations where corrosion may be a problem. Other steels are tough and do not shatter easily. Still others are resistant to different chemical reactions, or take a very sharp edge when honed like a knife or an arrowhead, or perform well in extreme heat or cold. The many differences in steel can be extreme.

Engineers working on 3D steel printing projects will have to suit their steel to their product, and their printing process to their steel. Steel with a high melting point will require adjustments to the laser that sinters the steel. Outstanding print engineers will understand the fine differences between the many alloys and know where to get them. They will know what they cost, how to store and handle them, and even what alloys can substitute for others if prices change or shortages occur. They will need all the skills any foreman or manager needs, but they will also need special scientific and mathematical knowledge.

One of the primary uses of 3D printing with steel is in high-speed prototyping in industries including aerospace and aviation design. In the early days of 3D printing, plastics were used for prototyping. This allowed designers to evaluate many elements of their designs but did not allow for direct testing of a finished product. Current metal-based printing changes that. It is now easy to design a machine part, or an entire machine, using computer-aided design, and use the design to generate a set of printing instructions. Once that is done, it is possible to print out the result in days, if not hours. A research team can test a result quickly and change the plan before anyone invests too much in a less-than-perfect solution.

That means that there's very little difference between prototype and actual finished product. Products for use and for sale are not very different from research models. The method and technology of the research phase is the same as the method and technology of the manufacturing phase.

In some ways, a factory worker will need some of the skills and knowledge needed by a researcher. Factory workers and quality-assurance engineers will need to understand the products they create and the flaws that could make them unsafe or useless. They will also have to understand how the 3D printing machines work, how they can fail, and how to fix problems as they develop. Workers in this type of factory will need at least some education in mechanics, engineering, and problem analysis.

Titanium

Titanium is another metal used in high-tech industry. It has special characteristics that make it a popular choice for many uses. It is a heat-resistant metal, melting only at very high temperatures. Like stainless steel, it resists rust and corrosion. It is tough and strong, hard to damage, and able to support great loads. It is very light and **ductile** at high temperatures. It is nontoxic and seldom triggers metal allergies. These traits make it very popular in medical uses, among others. It is as welcome in jewelry making as in aerospace, and it is used in glasses frames, fine pen tips, arts and crafts tools, and anywhere else a

Lili, a Chinese red-crowned crane, was given a 3D-printed prosthetic titanium beak to replace one damaged in a fight.

light, tough, flexible metal that takes a near-permanent polish could be used. It can be flexible enough that a thin strip can be bent into a loop, only to spring back to its own form. It is hard enough to mark glass. It is light enough that large, dangling earrings feel nearly weightless—and titanium earring hooks and posts do not irritate the piercings they pass through.

Since it became possible to print titanium objects, the metal has become particularly popular in medical and dental settings. All its characteristics work together to make it a great choice for implants of many types. Titanium pins can be used as anchors for artificial teeth, set into the bone of the jaw with a model tooth cemented to the pin. Titanium can replace missing bone or reinforce damaged bone. Pins of titanium serve to hold bones together when they're fractured. Doctors can design tailor-made replacements for missing portions of an accident victim's skull, providing a light but strong protection for the brain. The same metal can be used for crutches, canes, braces, and prostheses.

Production of titanium can be difficult, and learning about it can also be difficult. Titanium has many military uses as well as being used in the related aerospace and aeronautics industries. Information about supplies and processing can be classified. The metal is as important to our defense as iron was during past wars. It is not hard to see why—the same light, tough, strong traits that make it so useful elsewhere are useful in transportation, armor, and weaponry.

THE BIKE THAT TELLS THE FUTURE

It's easy to assume that people in business know pretty much how things are going to work in the future. They may not know perfectly, but they know pretty well. They know their own fields, so they know what is likely to happen next. Right?

The trouble is that there are times when so many things are changing that it can be hard to figure out what's coming next. This especially has been true the past two centuries, and things are not slowing down now. Every time people think we're over the hump and can relax and be stable for a little while, we hit another patch of change and we're all confused again. It's not just that we do not know for certain what new products are going to matter, what fads and fashions will come and go. We also do not know the best way to make the kinds of things we decide to make.

That is why Oved Valadez decided to build a bicycle: to try to figure out what products he might be making in the future and how he would be making them. Valadez is the founder of a company called Industry. It specializes in trying to help manufacturers, designers, and creators make intelligent choices about where things are going next in the world of industry. Valadez and his people try to guess the future—of style, of new products, and of manufacture. That's not easy to do when things are changing so quickly. The methods of production are changing very quickly as 3D printing becomes more and more common.

So Valadez decided to make a 3D-printed bicycle to explore how design, engineering, and manufacture worked together in the new world of 3D print production. It was intended as a project to test how a variety of different technologies and new patterns of team design worked together to create a finished product. Valadez is a designer himself, and he understands that the process of creating something affects the product you're creating.

The bicycle project was a test. Valadez and his team would use the latest collaborative software so they could share sketches, have interactive discussions, and use all the tools available to be a strong design team. They chose to use two modeling tools: cardboard mockups and 3D-printed test patterns. They decided that they wanted to manufacture the bike using 3D printing but do the finishing and detailing by hand. That allowed them to provide high-quality production and the artistry of hand craftsmanship, combining the excellence of two different skill sets.

In the end, Valadez and his team concluded that 3D printing was not yet up to the very highest standards they had hoped. There are problems with scaling and with quality of the printed product. They felt too much cleanup work was needed to provide a professional luxury finish. However, they also felt the entire system was the way of the future.

Because titanium is so light, it is very useful in any kind of travel application, and especially useful in air and space travel. It makes planes and rockets lighter, meaning they need less fuel. They are easier to steer, too—momentum is reduced when mass is reduced. A large, heavy object going at high speed is harder to turn than a large, light object going at high speed. Engineers love titanium—so many strengths, and it is light as well! Often there are tradeoffs in design. If a metal is strong, it is likely to be heavy. If armor is hard to pierce, it is a burden to wear. Titanium reduces these problems.

One challenge to working with titanium is its high melt point. Working with titanium means working with much higher temperatures than working with steel, just as steel means working at higher temperatures than working with most plastics.

Applications

Titanium can be used in almost any way that plastics or other metals can be used. You can make a light, tough bicycle frame using titanium. You can make decorative jewelry with titanium. You can produce light, sharp, flexible knife blades, or fan blades that will resist almost any impact from flying material striking them.

The metal and the machines for 3D printing with titanium are expensive and seldom available to the average student or hobby printer. However, at the university level or the corporate level, many more labs have access to both. College students and in-house engineers may have a chance to develop projects for themselves and for others using this material. Good project choices could include sports equipment, hunting equipment–including archery gear–jewelry, protective gear, prototyped vehicles, and more.

With the right equipment, titanium can be printed into weapons–a real concern in criminal or terrorist hands. New technologies come with benefits but also offer new and unexpected dangers. The ability to manufacture high-quality objects with ease opens many opportunities to ordinary people, but it also enables people we would rather not see given those chances. Titanium is used in cooking equipment because it is highly heat-resistant, nontoxic, and durable. It is used in automobile parts.

Aluminum

Aluminum is a common metal–the most common in Earth's upper crust. It is very light, nonmagnetic, and nontoxic. It can be polished to a high finish. It resists corrosion. In the first half of the twentieth century, aluminum was one of the metals associated with the most modern high-tech developments of the time. It was used in everything from household equipment to airplanes. Even now it is a common metal in high-tech applications.

Because it is already easy to machine into a wide range of shapes and forms, there's no major pressure to move to 3D printing for manufacture of larger aluminum products. However, in a different setting, and on a much smaller scale, aluminum is not only used in 3D printing, it is one of the most commonly printed metals. Aluminum is **conductive**; it carries electricity well. Because of this, it is one of the most desirable metals in electronics and computer design. Aluminum is used at all levels of computer design, from the tiniest elements of computer chips to the outer casing of laptops. It is possible to use 3D printing to design and manufacture computer chips and boards.

This complex, layered block shows the small-scale precision of microprinting.

Applications

The applications for aluminum are extensive, but their applications in 3D printing are largely limited to microprinting/nanoprinting. This printing is done on a scale so much smaller than ordinary 3D printing that it demands very different techniques. Nanoprinting lays down metals on a scale so small that the sizes are measured in microns, and the products made have to be observed through microscopes.

The filaments, beads, and powders used in larger-scale printing are not suited to nanoprinting. Laser light, however, remains a useful tool, and it is the key to the primary system used in this type of 3D printing, which is called **two-photon lithography**. The technique depends on a liquid plastic resin that sets only when exposed to two photons of light. There are a number of techniques that allow designers to build up resin, remove resin, and apply elements like aluminum to a product when the resin is impregnated with it. The aluminum remains conductive in the resin. This is a low-temperature way of laying down microscopic lines of aluminum in a resin base, allowing current to be carried on a molecular scale. Taken together, two-photon lithography offers all the tools necessary to print **dense**, complicated chips, nano devices, or many other microscopically scaled things.

It is in applications like this that aluminum comes into its own. It does not retain heat, it is light, and it is comparatively inexpensive. It is valued in the design of micro-technological devices. These can include medical tools, microscopic surgical devices, sensor tools–almost anything you think would be useful when working on a microscopic scale.

Precious and Semiprecious Metals

The precious and semiprecious metals most people associate with jewelry and coins are also used in 3D printing. Platinum, gold, silver, and copper are as useful as aluminum, particularly in small-scale electronics and computing applications. Here is a look at the characteristics of each of them.

- Platinum: This heavy, white metal resists corrosion and can take a high shine. Platinum is most commonly used for jewelry and decorative items. However, it also is used in medicine, dentistry, and computer design. It is an expensive metal, so it is used sparingly in any project. Even in jewelry, it is often used in ways that allow for hollow shells that appear solid, allowing less metal to be used than if the product were solid. It is denser than lead. It is malleable and easily formed. It is a good conductor of electricity.
- Gold: It is one of the original "noble metals," a term that refers to the fact that these metals do not easily rust or corrode. They are resistant to a range of chemical interactions, and so are

valued in settings where metals must survive challenging conditions. Gold is therefore used to protect more vulnerable metals, like copper, in electronics and computing applications.

- Silver: This metal does not resist corrosion as effectively as gold. It tarnishes, darkening and combining with oxygen to form a thin film on the surface of the metal. This reduces its value in many uses. However, it is a dense, solid material, and it is not as heavy as gold. It is easily worked—flexible and malleable, slow to crack when stretched thin. It is a great conductor of electricity. These traits make it popular in both the fabrication of jewelry and in electronics and computer design.
- Copper: This is the least expensive of the metals commonly associated with jewelry and the decorative arts. Copper is more often associated with electronics than jewelry. It is highly conductive, and it is less costly than gold or silver. These traits have made it one of the most popular metals for all electronic and computing uses.

Applications

The precious and semiprecious metals bridge the gap between large- and small-scale manufacture, being valued for their beauty and their utility.

PRODUCING PROSTHESES

Many older people remember when prostheses were barely better than Peg-Leg the Pirate's broomstick leg. Even the best prostheses made between World War II and the Vietnam War were long on attempts to "look natural" but short on improving mobility. Artificial legs were supportive. Those who needed them could walk on them. They were not as natural looking as hoped and not as useful as anyone dreamed.

Over the past decades, though, experimenting in the design of prostheses has expanded and come up with many answers to meet many needs. The ability to use 3D printing is part of this explosion. The result of access to 3D printing technology combined with better understanding of how a prosthesis can improve mobility has led to dozens of new prosthetic designs.

Some are beautiful—jet-black arabesque swirls of open work encasing empty space, artificial insteps that look like a stately knight's decorated sabbaton (foot shield), tangles of twining titanium rod racing between the knee and the ankle ... these prostheses are works of art. Their carefully considered joints and the form of their feet allow a wearer to move more normally.

Other prostheses are less artful—coarse, blockish hands that look like they were made of a child's extra-large snap construction blocks, in primary colors, connected by visible wires and held on by Velcro straps. It is difficult to imagine these are improvements for the people wearing them—until you watch a video of a child who can pick up a bottle of soda for the first time, or watch a toddler stand up cautiously, test his weight, and

This prosthetic hand is highly functional, and it comes with superhero styling.

then run, face shining with the sudden joy of freedom. Equally joyful are the classmates who helped print out the design and assemble it.

Both the artistic masterpieces and the simple but practical prostheses are gifts of 3D printing. The ugly prostheses are the result of the ability to cheaply manufacture missing hands and feet and legs for children young enough to be unable to afford a titanium work of art they'd need to resize every few months. The art prostheses, though, are also the result of affordability and ease of manufacture, allowing the designers who create them to take all the utility research has to offer and wrap it up in light, professionally produced, strong titanium, printed out easily on a laser-sintering printer.

There is never a good time to need a prosthesis. But this is a good time to get the prosthesis you need … no matter whether you need durable beauty or disposable utility.

Large-scale applications mainly consist of everything from jewelry to construction-sized electrical equipment. The wiring of houses, the switches and controls of appliances, and the insides of dashboards are all applications for large-scale metal projects.

The small scale is the microscale. These metals are well suited to many uses in electronics and computer design and manufacture. Even small devices like mobile phones and tablets contain chips and breadboards assembled using 3D print techniques with precious and semiprecious metals. As more and more appliances and tools are driven by electricity and controlled with computer elements, even items like electric rice cookers and automated devices are likely to contain microprinted components made with gold, copper, and silver.

Conclusion

Industry has use for all forms of 3D printing, but it is hard not to feel there is a special industrial sweet spot for the use of metals. We still associate metals with heavy industry, manufacturing, and international sale of North American products. The use of 3D printing to design, test, and manufacture high-tech products made of metal fits old and much-loved expectations about North American industrial health and growth. It allows North Americans to invent the technology, use it to create top-line products, and then manufacture them for a world market.

In this context, metals offer a great opportunity for North America to regain some of its lost manufacturing stature. The continent remains resource rich and has an educated labor pool that can do the research, take over the design and testing, and fill the manufacturing positions. There are many people who can be trained to use and maintain the 3D printing equipment. We have the aerospace industry, the aviation industry, the possibility of high-speed rail, and the renewal of automotive production to encourage the development of this technology on our own home soil.

The end products are excellent, the production runs uniform and consistent. The ability to produce optimal designs using strong, light materials leaves plenty of room for profit. Efficient, economical CAD design and 3D printing allow researchers to optimize material use to get the best product for the least cost. We can charge more for quality while spending less on materials. Or we can drop the price and make up for it in quantity of sales.

The same is true on the microprinting front. North America's computer designers still have the most creativity and training available, and 3D printing and nanoprinting keep us at the forefront of computer and electronics design and production. Even more than in heavy industry, though, designers using microprinting need strong educations in logic, scientific analysis, programming skills, and electronics design.

It's hard for people to shift their expectations regarding how to raise children and what education means to their future. For much of modern history, a person could reliably earn a respectable living with less than a high school education. Times have changed, though, and industry has changed with them. It's no longer possible to count on a job market with room for those with little education. Even if workers fail to complete college, it is now important for them to gain the skills in logic and technological understanding that would allow them to produce quality products using 3D printing methods.

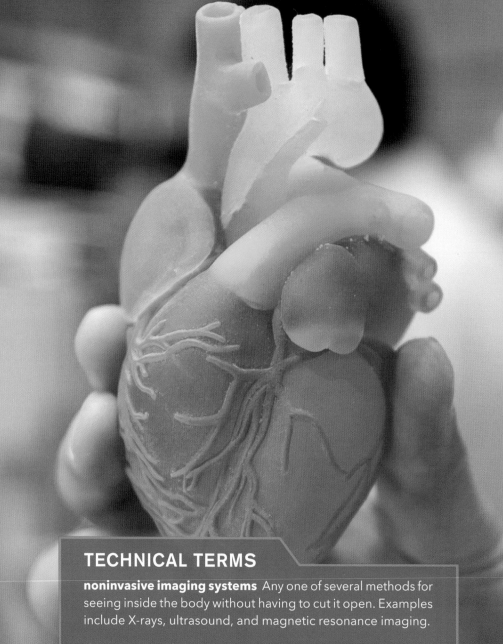

TECHNICAL TERMS

noninvasive imaging systems Any one of several methods for seeing inside the body without having to cut it open. Examples include X-rays, ultrasound, and magnetic resonance imaging.

tissue compatibility Just as blood types must match for safe transfusions, tissues must be compatible for transplants. This match is called tissue compatibility. The histocompatibility antigens (these trigger an immune response) of the donor and recipient must be a close match or there is greater chance of rejection of the donor tissue.

CHAPTER FOUR

Biomaterials

O F ALL THE FORMS OF 3D PRINTING, BIOPRINTING HAS TO be the most challenging and exciting, though it might be difficult to imagine without a strong medical background. Some of it is easy enough and has already been touched on: 3D printing allows doctors and surgeons to design replacements for damaged skulls using titanium, and to work out new ways of anchoring healing bones using biodegradable pins and plates that will disappear over time without the doctors having to remove them. These applications, though, are almost mechanical in comparison with some of the things bioprinting can do.

Opposite: With 3D printing, we can make exact replicas of individual human hearts.

The first thing to understand is that at some point bioprinting deals with living systems. Even a titanium implant must be safe to put in a human body. The metal may not be biological, but the body it will be implanted in is pure biology: alive, built of living cells.

But there is bioprinting that goes beyond that: bioprinting using living cells and nutrient solutions as inks, laying down layers of cells separated by molecule-thin layers of water, building structures that will then grow together and become a living system, or a superb forgery of a living system.

Bioprinting creates models of organs so real they can be used to educate students without sacrificing actual people or animals. It can create models so real that surgeons and their teams can use the printed product to rehearse actual surgeries, as discussed in chapter 1.

Bioprinting can go further, providing working synthetic skin available to treat burn victims. Burning remains one of the most painful and dangerous types of injury. Mortality rates for burn victims are higher than in almost any other type of accident. The loss of skin causes a large part of the problem, opening the body to infection and leaving nerves exposed to pain. The ability to replace missing skin in any way improves survival rates. Artificial printed skin gives doctors a resource that saves lives, makes later healing and repair much easier, and reduces scarring that would require reconstructive surgery.

Researchers have recently found ways to reproduce **collagen** and **fibrin**, which are tissues that help knit your muscles and organs together. They can also reproduce cartilage, the rubbery, tough, plastic-like material in your ears and nose that also cushions the ends of your bones. The ability to print out new caps for joints using synthetic cartilage will help keep many people out of slings, off of crutches and canes, and out of wheelchairs.

There are hybrid forms of bioprinting, too. Imagine using a biodegradable plastic to provide a skeleton on which to build an organ—let's say a liver. There has to be some kind of skeleton to hold it all together, after all. You'd build a lacy liver-shaped 3D web using PLA plastic that would eventually be absorbed into the body. Then you'd build onto the scaffold, using bioinks to introduce connective tissue cells and liver cells, hoping in time they would knit together. You'd print out blood vessels. Finally, you would add layers of tissue to contain the liver, along with layers of PLA to hold the new organ together until it all grew into a single new liver.

That's not yet possible, but there is every reason to think it soon will be. Progress so far has shown we can use combinations of biodegradable materials and natural cells to create living, functioning organs. They're not yet up to being used in transplants, but the remaining problems look like they can be solved.

Think of what that will mean to medicine. Right now we have people on transplant lists who will die long before they get matched with an organ. In the future, it is possible that as soon as they are diagnosed, doctors can start growing them a new organ. If they are sick because of injury or damage, their own cells can be used to grow a new one. If the organ failure is genetic, the genes can be "fixed," and the new organ will be so close to identical that there will be no rejection–but also no defects. In the time it takes to grow a new organ, the patient can be cured, without any of the problems of **tissue compatibility**.

Bioprinting offers some of the most amazing possibilities of all 3D printing because it works with the material of life itself. It can heal injuries, change lives for the better, and make things possible that are currently impossible.

Biomodeling

Biomodeling creates near-real models of living parts. Where many other forms of 3D printing start with a design, biomodeling starts with tests and imaging procedures. This is because biomodeling is based on real things that already exist. Instead of imagining what is to be printed out, people study what they want to print a copy of. To study, they use noninvasive imaging systems.

Noninvasive imaging systems are the many testing methods we have developed that allow us to "look into" the body without having to cut into it, or do other sorts of damage. The earliest of these techniques was the X-ray. Since then, the techniques have expanded, until now they include CT (computed tomography) scans, which are an advanced form of X-ray; MRI (magnetic

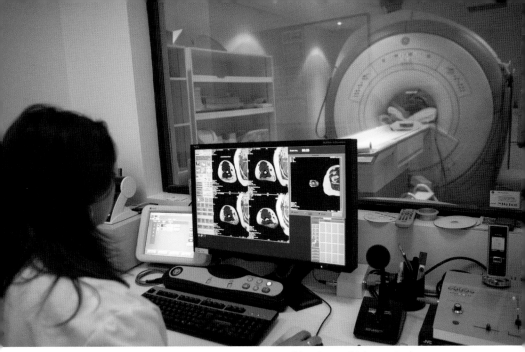

An MRI machine shows cross sections of bodies, which can be used to print accurate models.

resonance imaging) scans, which use magnetic and radio signals; and ultrasound, which uses sound waves to see, much the way bats and dolphins use sonar. All of these can be used to get a two-dimensional picture of something, looking down at one plane of the body, or they can be used to build 3D images of the body by "slicing" over and over, each slice a new picture on a transparency. The transparencies can then be piled up to show a 3D image, and then unstacked to let the doctor or researcher see a particular frame of the picture.

These noninvasive techniques have been improved to the point of near-microscopic precision, with doctors able to see very fine detail. It is like a multilevel floor plan for every single detail of a human body, or part of a body. You can examine a heart, a brain, or a kidney.

Or you can remove a printed heart, a brain, or a kidney and do the same kind of noninvasive examination of an organ, getting finer resolution. Again, it makes a blueprint of a human organ.

That blueprint is part of what makes 3D bioprinting possible. Because the image is so perfect, and because we've spent several centuries investigating human tissues and organs, we can then use the blueprint to put together a false organ that is almost perfect, and is quite perfect enough for students to study or surgeons to practice on.

The false models are built in layers, just as the scans were made in layers. The materials are a hybrid of actual living cells in bioinks and plastics that can replace connective tissue and help provide form and strength for the model. The final version includes everything that was found using the tests. If the model is of a human brain with a brain tumor, it will show how that tumor is woven through and around the blood vessels, and where it has progressed into the brain itself. If it is a model of a damaged heart, it will include the damaged valves, the clogged arteries, and every other detail of one particular, specific, unique organ.

The blueprint can last as long as it needs to. It is a digital plan that can be stored on digital media. It can be used to make one heart—or a hundred identical hearts, just like the original heart. Every student in a biology classroom can have the same heart, for fairness—or every student can have a different heart, from a different blueprint, recorded at a different time, allowing the class to see many heart conditions in one lab. You can print as many different blueprints as you want, or you can print one blueprint over and over, as many times as you need to understand what the problems are and how to fix them.

Applications

There are many applications for this technology when it is fully mature. The example of supplying students with samples for study is one obvious case, but students are not the only people who need to study organs.

Corporations in pharma, cosmetics, chemicals, and other specialized fields all have need of test material to make sure their products are safe. Biomodeling offers the possibility of testing on nonliving but fully human materials, sparing both humans and animals from some types of testing. As biomodeling improves and model organs come closer and closer in quality to transplantable organs, this function will become more popular. Scientists have always known that the most accurate model for human tissue is human tissue. Everything else is an imperfect match. That means every other test subject leaves room for mistakes.

Corporations do not like to make mistakes if there is an easy way to avoid them. The ability to check the safety of their products on "real" human tissue for low prices will encourage the use of biomodel test subjects.

Biomodels are already used for rehearsal of surgery. Because of the ability to reproduce the same model multiple times, surgeons can analyze their own performance. They can look for ways to improve and for quicker techniques that will put less strain on patients. They can try to spot potential difficulties ahead of time, so they will know if veins pass in unusual ways, or if minor mutations or birth defects have led to nonstandard conformation. All these things lead to safer surgeries and more successful outcomes.

Biomodeling also contributes to the more distant goal of producing organs for transplant and artificial body parts for reconstructive surgery. Biomodeling itself is not intended to replace human transplant material. The aim is to provide a good forgery, not an actual substitute. But the skills gained in learning how to make a good forgery can then be used to learn how to make a new, living organ. Creating biomodels using 3D printing is a form of research, letting scientists and doctors explore new ways of using bioprinting.

Bioscaffolds

Bioscaffolds are used in a different way from biomodeling, with different goals. Biomodels are intended to be used as models of human parts. Bioscaffolding is using 3D printing to create skeletons and frames to support new, growing, living human parts.

The problem with "printing" an organ is knitting the living cellular material together strongly enough to hold everything together as a whole. The layers the

These are 3D-printed bioscaffolds that can support further layers of 3D bioprinting with living cells.

printer puts down are not stuck together with the strong connective tissues real human organs have. One of the ways to make sure new, living organs would have that connective tissue is to let them grow their own. That would mean printing out living human organ cells that will grow and divide and spread. They will also grow their own supportive material. But until they do, the shape they need can be provided by a scaffold.

This is a bit like a clay sculptor building an armature to support the clay as a statue is built. Armatures are rough supports made of a variety of materials. They only provide a rigid structure to keep the soft clay from collapsing.

The challenge to creating bioscaffolds is to create something soft and light enough to accept bioinks of living cells, but strong and rigid enough to hold their

PIONEERS OF BIOPRINTING

As a new technology, bioprinting doesn't have much of a history, and everyone working in the field qualifies as a "pioneer." Here are a few outstanding figures in the field, though.

Professor Makoto Nakamura studied at Kobe University in Japan and went on to work as a research

Professor Makoto Nakamura, who pioneered bioprinting, shows off his original printer.

assistant at the National Cardiovascular Center in Japan, developing artificial hearts. Over time he became dissatisfied with the limits imposed by mechanical solutions to heart transplants, and he shifted his studies to tissue engineering. One day he recognized that inkjet printers had cartridges and ink feeds almost the same size as human blood cells. Over a period between 2005 and 2008, he organized a bioprinting project in collaboration with the Kanagawa Academy of Science and Technology. By 2008, the project had successfully redesigned and retooled the first printer to allow experimentation in bioprinting.

Jemma Redmond was a physicist trained at the Robert Gordon University in Aberdeen, Scotland. She obtained an advanced degree in nano-bioscience from University College Dublin in Ireland. She founded an Irish biotech company called Ourobotics. She developed the first ten-material bioprinter able to handle living human cells. She also developed a robotic arm able to handle ten materials for use in manipulating elements in bioprinting. She died unexpectedly in 2016, at the age of thirty-eight. Her company and her accomplishments have survived her.

shape, even as the organ grows. Scientists are using a range of materials. Good materials for bioscaffolding have to be biocompatible, with a permeable structure that can be penetrated by growing cells as they knit themselves into a solid organ. They need to be cost effective–if the materials are too expensive, they make the growth of artificial organs impractical.

Scientists are using a range of natural materials for bioscaffolds. Some use bioplastics, including the biodegradable PLA plastic mentioned in chapter 2. Others are focusing on collagen and fibrin–natural connective tissue that holds living bodies together. A wide range of gels are being explored.

There are two stages of 3D bioprinting with bioscaffolding techniques. The first stage is the production of the scaffold. Researchers must decide on the shape, size, and thickness of the scaffold. They need a scaffold strong enough to do its job, but not so thick or clumsy as to damage a working organ like a heart. Once the scaffold has been designed and then printed, the second stage begins, as scientists use cartridges of bioinks to build up a living layer of cells, which are intended to then grow in place on the scaffold.

There is some experimentation under way using bioscaffolds as bases for reconstructive surgery. With the new ability to generate cartilage, features like ears and noses can be replaced using natural, biocompatible materials. This is especially important for extremely disfigured victims of fire, violence, or accidental injury who have lost their natural faces. While there is progress in replacing faces with transplanted faces harvested from the dead, it would be more ideal to make natural repairs using fully compatible biomaterials including scaffolding of cartilage, collagen, and fibrin, along with other biomaterials, to sculpt a new face with no possibility of rejection.

Applications

Applications for bioscaffolding focus primarily on two areas: the growth of transplantable organs and body parts, and the ability to use bioscaffolding to improve the outcome of reconstructive surgery. That does not mean there are no other possible uses for bioscaffolding. However, these are the most immediately obvious concerns.

Bioscaffolding is in use in cartilage and bone regeneration. It is also used to help regenerate skin on burn victims—the gels used are layered over the injury and seeded with living skin cells, serving as a growth medium for new, healthy layers of living skin.

Permeable and biodegradable materials are used as bone substitutes when bones are so badly damaged that there are bits missing. The scaffolding material will be seeded with bone cells and inserted in place to fill in the empty space. Either the scaffold must be strong enough to carry weight temporarily, or there must be other support supplied.

Over time, as people become more expert at creating and using these printed supports and all the other techniques of bioengineering, scaffolds are expected to be used in many other operations, improving healing and reducing collateral damage from operations and other treatments.

Bioinks

Bioinks are liquid and semiliquid mixes of biological and nonbiological ingredients that are used in bioprinting. There are many possible bioinks, and more are in development. Bioinks can be laid down in filaments, like strings of toothpaste, or sprayed in a wide layer over an existing growth medium.

These printing materials are usually made with a base of some gelatinous substance to provide a substance to hold living cells. The gels provide a secure support for seeded cells, providing room to grow and multiply, and a stable environment to grow in. Common gels used for bioinks are made of a range of different natural substances. Alginate is a form of sugar. Gelatin is approximately the same animal-based gel you encounter in school lunches or as dessert. Gelatin is made from the connective tissues of animals, including skin, cartilage, and bones. Bioinks are also made from a gel called decellularized ECM. This can be made of almost any mammalian cell source that has been stripped of its nucleus to remove genetic material and then gelatinized. Another gel used in bioinks is made from poloxamer, a complex copolymer.

Bioinks feature living cells intended to grow either freeform or on scaffolds. When they are grown freeform, they may be printed in a single layer, or they may be printed in multiple layers separated by layers of sterile water. Researchers seed the cells they want to grow in the gels they've chosen. They can then be placed in a holding cartridge and extruded as a biofilament.

Bioinks are used in almost all forms of bioprinting. They and other materials used in bioprinting require growth environments consistent with any other living substance. They are treated differently than any other 3D printing material. Temperatures must be in a narrow range compatible with human survival. They must be kept moist, and living cells must be fed if they are to survive. Growth hormones may be added to nutrient baths to encourage cell division and expansion. Light is limited, though not ruled out.

Conclusion

The knowledge needed to fully understand bioprinting is too advanced for most people. The imagination needed to understand the power of this 3D printing technology is not. As impressive and important as other forms of 3D printing are, few will have the impact on the world that bioprinting will. More people are likely to find jobs printing out metal-based products on 3D printers. More will become product designers, or develop prostheses, or become artists using 3D printing to execute complicated, difficult creations in ceramics, metals, and plastics. Relatively few will become bioprinting technicians, and fewer still will become the researchers, doctors, and scientists who will use this technology to change the world.

That does not mean the power of the technology is anything less than amazing. Right now bioprinting has barely started. The first bioprinting machine was only developed in 2008, about a decade before the writing of this book. Since that time, though, the field has gone from first thought to offering life-saving techniques and products to the world. Another twenty years are likely to bring printable transplant organs, treatments for severe injuries, and a way to repair dozens of medical problems. Of all the technologies in development at this time, only genetic manipulation is likely to be more powerful.

There will be new jobs arising from the new technology. Many different technician specialties will open up as more and more of the process of design and production is stabilized. Mechanical experts to improve and maintain bioprinting machines will be needed. Biodesigners will work to develop individual designs for people who have been injured or who suffer from physical defects. Reconstructive designers will work with surgeons and plastic surgeons to give people new faces and new body parts after severe injury.

The change in health will be the biggest change, though. As of the spring of 2017, there were more than ninety-three thousand people waiting for kidneys on the US Kidney Transplant List. There were nearly seventeen

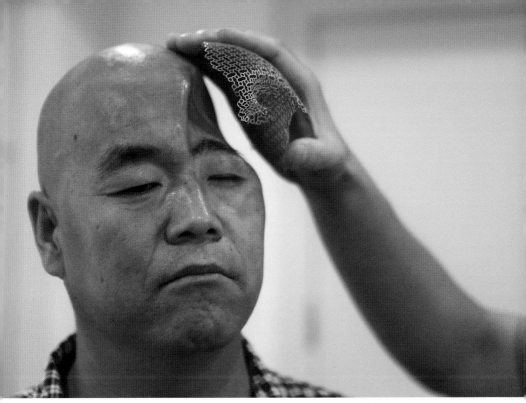

This patient in China was fitted with a 3D-bioprinted replacement for a caved-in skull section.

thousand waiting for new livers. More than two thousand needed a new pancreas. Twenty-two people were dying per day waiting for an organ. The list goes on and on.

That doesn't even take into account people whose lives would be improved by the ability to receive new, better organs than those they started with. Women who would otherwise be barren could have new, healthy ovaries grown or could replace wombs lost to cancer with new wombs grown from their own cells.

That does not even begin to account for all the possibilities. Only time will show us all the things this technology could offer and how many lives it could improve and extend.

TECHNICAL TERMS

slurry A wet blend of solids and liquids.

veneer A thin strip of one material, often intended to be used to put a new surface over another material.

vitrify To melt a ceramic substance until it forms a glassy bond. Not all ceramic substances can be vitrified.

CHAPTER FIVE

Unusual Materials

ALONG WITH ALL THE STANDARD AND HIGH-TECH MATERIALS and uses for 3D printing, there are a growing number of less recognized possibilities. Anything that can be built using materials in additive layers can be adapted to some form of 3D printer.

The limits are wide. Think about all the uses already discussed: Plastics can be printed using filaments that are melted and applied in layers, beads that are spread out in layers and then sintered using lasers, or liquid resins that are cured using UV lasers. Metals are powdered and formed in powder beds much like plastic beads, or are fed as ultrafine wire, melted at high heats,

Opposite: A 3D printer was used to create this pop-art sculpture of a spilling tomato soup can.

and applied to the printer bed or to the previous layers in a constant series of microwelds. Bioinks are fed, as gels, onto scaffolds or layered over each other with thin sheets of water maintaining some separation between layers.

To accomplish 3D printing, you need something that can be applied in small, precise amounts to preplanned layers. Your material has to be compatible with some machine that will feed your material out, a bit at a time. You need some way to make sure your material will become solid enough to hold its shape. Other than that, though, there are no limits. Anyone who wanted could, for example, develop a printer to create sculpted nail polish decorations, or invent a device based on a hot glue gun to squeeze out layers of glue in ornate patterns. Anything that can be applied with a "printer" that builds things out of layers of material added together to make one object may be counted as part of the 3D printing movement.

Right now, many people are doing things with 3D printing that are not widely known or recognized. Some are high-tech. Some are industrial. Some are artistic, and others are aimed at hobby printers. They offer all sorts of unexpected or unusual materials.

Ceramics

You can use clay and high-tech industrial ceramics in 3D printers to produce art or machine parts as durable as steel.

Ceramics cover a family of materials that all have a few things in common: they're not metal, they are not carbon, and when heated, they fuse together, forming a solid shape. The most common ceramic most of us are familiar with is clay—but even clay is more varied than most people realize. Porcelain, for example, is made from the mineral kaolinite. Stoneware contains traces of kaolinite but is also made of mica and quartz. Earthenware fuses but does not **vitrify**—develop into a glassy mass that shatters along a clean line, like porcelain and, to a lesser degree, stoneware. Each has a different composition, containing different minerals. All are called ceramics.

High-tech ceramics are made of a wide range of vitrifying minerals. Silicon nitride is used for durable ball bearings. Ceramic knives are made of zirconium dioxide. Ceramics have been made using boron carbide, alumina, silicon carbide, steatite, cordierite, and mullite. Each mineral has its own traits, though as a group they share many traits in common.

High-tech ceramics offer pros and cons in use. They've been considered for engine parts in rockets and race cars: they do not warp, they are tough and hard, and they are slow to wear down. However, like more familiar ceramics used daily, or like glass, when they do break, they shatter. A ceramic knife blade is strong, takes a fine edge, and will stay sharp far longer than steel—but unlike steel, it has no flex, and if you drop it, it can snap. But at the same time, high-tech ceramics can resist shattering in the face of amazing forces. Ceramics are used in bulletproof vests; they are as durable as bulletproof glass and as slow to break. Like titanium, ceramics are core high-tech materials used in 3D printing, and research into ways of using ceramics is a hot field of development.

High-tech ceramics have also become popular with jewelry designers for many of the same reasons they are

3D printing is equally adaptable to art as to technology, as this delicate eggcup shows.

liked in industry. The materials are beautiful and can easily be formed into elegant, sensual designs. They take a high polish and can bond with precious metals. They are durable, light, and hypoallergenic. Black and dark-gray ceramics offer an imposing look that many men find beautiful without being feminine. Watchbands and rings are common items of ceramic jewelry.

Artists use 3D printing machines to shape both high-tech and more ordinary clays. Using CAD programs and slicing software, they develop designs that take full advantage of the medium, producing many elegant, airy sculptures that are both representational and abstract. The medium of 3D-printed ceramics has already stopped being mere novelty art. The artists using these methods work to a very high standard.

The advantage of combining CAD design and 3D-printed production means that artists can produce whatever they can imagine, within the physical capacity of the material, without fear of clumsy hands making a mistake or a weary mind becoming confused as they work. The techniques permit enormous control. The finished works include many looks. Some seem organic, like art made of lacy seaweed, feathers, or flowers. Others seem pristine and mechanical, or geometric. Some artists favor the natural white of the ceramic itself. Others choose to color their completed works. There is so much variety that only their perfect, flawless technique marks them as being made using computers and printers, rather than human hands.

Paper

Paper is an unusual material for 3D printing, yet many people are exploring the possibilities presented. Papier-mâché has been a popular material for art and furnishings for more than two centuries, and layered **veneers** of organic products are strong and widely used. In that context, 3D printing with paper becomes a bit less strange.

Mcor Technologies Ltd., an Irish company, is one of the large companies using 3D printing techniques with paper. Its machines are designed to cut and layer paper, gluing the layers together as they go. The finished result is similar to plywood, composite bamboo flooring, or stacked veneers. The results are beautiful and effective. The company has produced 3D topographical representations of geological features and models of historic buildings. The layers of paper form subtle terracing effects where the product slopes, with each layer showing a step up or down.

Mcor Technologies is also able to produce practical items, such as tailor-made packaging for products, cases for phones and tablets, prototypes, storage containers, and other things. Almost anything you'd want to make of wood or cardboard can be made from Mcor's paper-based 3D printing process.

Other companies make packaging not by printing but by using forms made using 3D printing. A Chinese company that produces tailor-made packaging out of paper pulp rather than with finished paper sheets came to Stratasys with a problem. This company made its packaging by dipping a metal tool into a paper pulp **slurry** that can be altered to suit a project, adding glues and inks to alter rigidity and color. The tool served as a kind of form, and one was needed for each project. The cost of designing and making the metal tools was too high. A division of Stratasys came up with a way to design and print forms using fused deposition modeling, or FDM. The forms make prototyping of products much faster, and the process costs 98 percent less than traditional metal tooling. Also, the printed forms work better than the metal tools.

Applications

Paper offers almost infinite uses, particularly if used in conjunction with well-chosen glues, resins, glazes, and suspensions. Just as layered, veneered wood can be stacked and glued to create a longer, stronger beam than nature could produce, layered, veneered paper can be rigid, durable, water and fire resistant, and attractive. Paper is suited to decoration. It can take inks and paints well, both before production and after.

Construction

One of the least publicized areas of development in 3D printing includes new machines and techniques aimed at building construction, and not small-scale building construction, either. In China, huge 3D construction printers are already being used to build entire houses, and China is one of the primary places this technology is being developed. China produced the first functional 3D-printed house in 2016, over a period of forty-five days. The Chinese have since gone on to plan and execute other 3D-printed buildings. In one case, a ten-house development was built over the course of a single day. The construction printers use concrete as their building medium.

In March of 2017, the Dubai-based construction company Cazza announced its intention to build the world's first 3D-printed skyscraper. It intends to use a system it calls "crane printing," which uses standard cranes with minimal modifications. The materials used will be concrete and steel.

In the United States, Apis Cor uses its own crane system to print out small concrete houses in a day or less. Apis Cor estimates the cost to produce a 400-square-foot (37.2-square-meter) house is approximately $10,000. It has suggested the houses could be used to provide shelter for those left homeless by natural disasters. Given the popularity of the tiny house movement, the same designs may be used by people wanting to downsize.

Those are not the only designs possible, though, nor are Dubai, China, or Apis Cor's machines the only possible 3D construction printers. Concrete is a good

This housing development in China shows what 3D printing can do in the field of construction.

choice for 3D-printed housing, but other possibilities could be explored.

Applications

The ability to produce buildings using 3D printing techniques and concrete printing materials opens up many possibilities not yet explored. On the one hand, it infringes on many construction jobs traditionally done by human workers. On the other, it shifts the burden of labor away from the physical work of framing, moving it to the areas of design and all the many fine finishing details. In the meantime, the new technique offers the possibility of secure, affordable housing for minimal cost, using commonplace materials.

The scale ranges from the small–sheds and storage units–to enormous skyscrapers like the one being considered in Dubai. Housing developments could be put up in weeks–or days. Outbuildings like barns, workshops, and garden sheds can be put up easily and quickly, and the results will be sturdy, secure, and long lasting. In many ways, this approach to building could offer more substantial housing for the world than the wood-frame buildings commonly put up in the United States.

Other Materials and Uses

Many other industries and hobbies are making use of 3D printing, using many different materials. Some of the following are examples of the creativity and diversity of the uses people have found for the new technology.

Wax Jewelry

Jewelry can be made with 3D printing techniques using metals like steel and titanium or high-tech ceramics. 3D printing, however, can also expand on the ways older methods are used. Lost-wax casting is one of the oldest methods of metalworking, used for thousands of years to create complicated three-dimensional forms in metal. Jewelers and fine craft artisans continue to use lost-wax casting today. The method is so useful it is unlikely to ever be lost.

There are many advantages to creating wax models for lost-wax casting using a 3D printer. The first is that by using CAD programs and 3D printers, it is possible to create extremely detailed, precise models of complex shapes that would be difficult or even impossible to produce using older handmade methods. There is no need to keep copies of master molds to manufacture the models, either. The phrase "they broke the mold when she was made" helps explain what is involved in old wax casting. A model would be hand-sculpted. It would then be used to create a master mold, intended to create more models. The master mold would be saved carefully, because every wax model used in lost-wax casting is destroyed in the process of producing a metal piece of jewelry. To make a consistent line of cast works, you need to use the master mold to reproduce the model over and over again. If the mold is broken, it is no longer possible to make exact replicas of the original model. There are only two times when a jeweler "breaks the mold." One is by accident; the second is when he or she decides to stop producing the piece of jewelry forever. This is often done with limited-run art. It is also done with customized pieces sold as unique. To ensure that no one will ever have a piece of jewelry exactly the same as the commissioned piece, the mold is broken once a finished piece is completed and accepted by the client.

With a CAD program and a 3D printer, there is no "mold." There is a design, recorded digitally, and a slicer program that guides the printer to make the wax

PRINTING THAT'S LIGHTER THAN AIR

There are many materials available for printing, but few are as strange as graphene aerogel, the lightest material on Earth. This material is a deceptively smoke- or cloudlike substance that looks like it should be a vapor. The aerogel is really a solid, with interesting attributes.

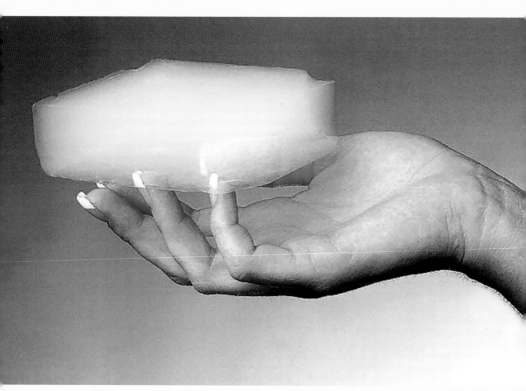

This graphene aerogel, as translucent as mist, was printed on a scaffold of ice.

Scientists have been studying aerogels for some time out of interest in their unusual properties. Graphene aerogel is likely to be a popular choice for study, though, as a way has been discovered to produce it using a 3D printer. The process, which consists of several stages, including the addition of water to the original sample of graphene, ends with the resulting gel built up over scaffolds of ice, in a process related to that of laying down bioinks over scaffolds of cartilage. After the structure is formed, the scaffold must be removed, leaving the aerogel behind—a blob so mysterious and strange that it seems like science fiction.

The end result of the process is the ability to produce consistent, uniform units of a substance lighter than air. That makes it far easier for students and faculty members to commit to research by making the material reliable and easy to obtain. The aerogel has peculiar properties that may have use in any number of real-world applications. Some seem downright odd, such as invisibility cloaks. Others are more common: NASA used aerogel as thermal insulation on the Mars Rover and in space suits.

model. The digital file takes up no room. If it is backed up properly, the pattern can't be lost. Even if it is lost, a finished piece of jewelry can be visually analyzed and converted into a new pattern. Variations can be made, stored together, and none of the old process of making the first model and mold is necessary.

Therefore, many jewelers are now using this method to develop and manage their own lost-wax designs. Other 3D printing companies are offering their services to jewelers, giving them alternate ways to manage their creations.

Metals, LEDs, and Wearable Technology

Another form of jewelry being made today is strictly high-tech: wearable electronic and computing art. The same 3D printing techniques used to make computer chips and breadboards can also be used to create complex, three-dimensional jewelry and costume pieces, using conductive metals, LEDS, and computer control chips.

Food

Chefs and restaurateurs have discovered the 3D printer, too. The machines allow them to combine the advantages of fresh cooking on site with the consistency and polished, manufactured appearance of factory-made items. In a business where flavor and appearance vie with each other on every plate, 3D printing is a great addition to the chef's toolbox of techniques.

Chefs care about presentation. A neat plate with beautiful food pleases the customer and sets off the quality of the chef's skill. Top chefs prefer that every dish tastes fantastic, and looks just as fantastic.

Chefs also care about consistency in all things. Customers want to trust that what they ordered last week will taste the same next week, and that what they ordered is not better or worse than the same dish on their neighbor's plate. A beautiful professional presentation and constant appearance help create that kind of client confidence.

That ideal is achievable using 3D printers. The growing selection of printers designed specifically for printing food can create slick, professional-looking products, including baked goods, chocolate and icing decorations, and baked pastry baskets in which to present other foods. These printers come with nozzles of many shapes and with food canisters to hold a range of different preparations.

Using these items, even chefs with limited presentation skills of their own can produce food that looks professional and elegant.

Specialty and Mimic Filaments, PLA

Among the kinds of PLA filaments offered are some novelty and mimic fibers, developed to provide a number of special effects. An example of a specialty filament would be PLA blended with short lengths of carbon fiber. This filament creates a very rigid material. There is PLA made with powdered bronze included, which produces

SWEET 3D PRINT PROJECTS

Among the more appealing substances to print out using a 3D printer is candy. There are many applications for food-based printing being developed all the time, and candy printing is a tempting choice for many people.

These delicate chocolate objects printed on a 3D printer are art you can eat.

Students at the University of Connecticut have chocolate printing as a class project. The work is designed to make them solve multiple problems to get a good result. They have to learn the skills of the chocolatier, the designer, and the print manager to complete their assignment. The challenge is not small. To produce a perfect result, chocolate must be handled at the right temperatures. It must be liquid enough to flow. It must be hot enough not to lose its temper, but cool enough to be shaped as the printer pumps out a slow, thick stream of chocolate. If the chocolate is to be more than one layer, the layers must be at the right point between cool and hot to bond successfully.

The printer must be ready to process the chocolate. The printer bed must be prepped and ready for a build. Each of these details requires advance research and planning. The UConn students can't just toss a chocolate bar at the machine and expect a good outcome.

They're not the only people dreaming sweet dreams with 3D printers, though. In 2014, the Sugar Lab at 3D Systems, a company specializing in 3D printing, developed techniques for printing out fancy sugar, from geometric designs to delicate filigree skulls perfect for a Día de los Muertos party. The company was selling both the 3D food printer to make the candy sculptures and the sugar art.

a bronzed metallic surface—a strong visual effect that adds style and dignity to finished forms. Mimic materials imitate wood, sandstone, and marble, as well as offering other visual effects.

Conclusion

There are more materials used in 3D printing, and more will be added every year. The technology is too useful and adaptable for anything else to be true. As uses expand and materials multiply, this form of manufacturing and construction will become a common element in our homes, just as computers and computer printers have become common.

That will change our world, in particular the worlds of education and of employment preparation. While 3D printing is unlikely to take away all the jobs in the world, it will change the things people will want to learn to prepare for those jobs. Just as carpenters must train to use power saws, everyone these days needs to be able to use a computer to at least some degree, and people are going to need to be able to run a 3D printer. For most people, that will involve basic knowledge of plastics printers, as these are the most likely to be used in daily life. For people who want to go into aerospace or high-tech manufacturing, though, it may be necessary to learn how to use specialized industrial printers. People going into medicine at any level may want to become familiar with the uses of bioprinters.

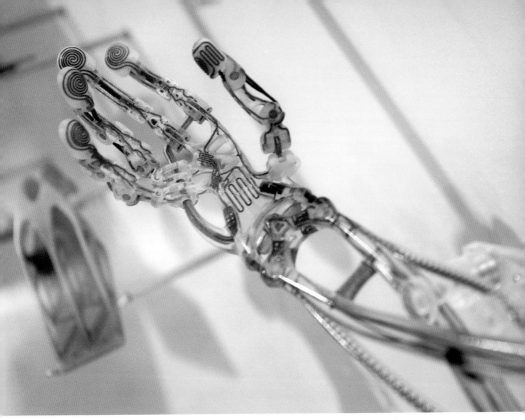

Research and development in 3D printing may lead to prostheses with a sense of touch.

The more powerful way these printers will change our lives is through the creative ways they will provide new possibilities. Printed buildings will become more common, and creative people will find millions of uses for them. Bioprinting will offer health choices never available before and improve outcomes in transplant surgery, medical implants, and reconstructive medicine. The handy plastics printer many people will have in the household will make it easy for people to manufacture their own tools and devices. Designing and manufacturing your own tools, furniture, and decorative objects may become so popular and convenient that it will become a common hobby, like woodworking, knitting, or sewing.

This kind of flexible power has an enormous effect on how people experience their own lives. People throughout time have loved the feeling of self-sufficiency and control. The new 3D printer technology offers improved levels of control for almost everyone.

Right now, specialists design and manufacture prostheses. Soon, with strong educational training and a 3D printer, people who use prostheses may be able to design and manufacture their own, creating their own idea of the "best" prosthesis for their activities and their own needs.

There are tools that increase your power in the world. A hammer lets you hit a nail harder than you could with your fist, or even with a rock. A car lets you travel faster and farther than you could on your own feet or when riding a horse. A computer with an internet connection ties you to the world. To increase your control of your world and life with these things, all you need to do is to train in the skills to use them well. A carpenter learns to drive a nail. A driver learns to drive a car, takes tests, and gets a license. A computer user develops the skills needed to use a computer for his or her own goals—whether that means learning to use a word processor or to stream movies. Training in STEM and related fields will make it easier to later use 3D printers well. These machines open doors to an exciting future.

GLOSSARY

acrylonitrile butadiene styrene (ABS) A petrochemical-based plastic; the most commonly used plastic in 3D printing.

additive manufacturing (AM) Another name for 3D printing. Because all 3D printing methods involve creating an object through the addition of material in layers, the methods are called AM.

biocompatible Material that, when used in a transfusion or a transplant, can work with the biological material of the recipient without causing damage.

biodegradable Anything that will break down into harmless chemicals on exposure to heat, light, and water, or molds, fungus, and bacteria.

bioinks Complex formulas for bioprinting, made from a variety of substances plus living cells, used to build up model organs or to do research aimed at reproducing organs and body parts. Bioinks are layered over scaffolding or layered over other bioinks, with only thin layers of water separating the layers.

bioprinting The use of a bioprinter to create biological models and scaffolds, and to reconstruct organs and body parts for experimentation in creating working human organs for transplant.

collagen A protein that helps hold the body together. It forms a scaffold within bones, muscle, skin, and tendons to give them strength and structure.

computed tomography (CT) scan A method of taking sequential X-rays to see crosscut slices of the human body. It is a noninvasive imaging technique.

computer-aided design (CAD) Designing with the help of a computer software program. It can design in 3D and provide views from all angles.

conductive A material that can carry an electrical current.

dense A large mass packed into a small space. Packed ice cream is dense; whipped cream is not.

direct metal laser sintering (DMLS) A 3D printing method that bonds together bits of metal, in powder or bead form, one layer at a time, using a precise laser to generate the necessary heat.

ductile Easily drawn out into a long, thin wire.

extruded Thrust or forced out through a small opening, as toothpaste is extruded from a tube.

fibrin A protein that forms a mesh during clotting to stop the flow of blood.

filament A thin thread, fiber, or cord.

fused deposition modeling (FDM) One of the earliest and most common methods of 3D printing, particularly popular for plastics. A filament or wire is fed through a guide nozzle with a heating element. The plastic or metal is heated until it just reaches the melting point and is laid down in layers that fuse together. "Deposition" means "to deposit." The name refers to deposited material fused together into the form of a model.

high-impact polystyrene (HIPS) This is polystyrene (a plastic) that is impact-resistant. It is popular for 3D printing when low-strength but impact-resistant projects are planned.

hot end The part of a 3D printer that includes the filament feed/nozzle and the heating element that melts the material. It is named for the heating element.

hydroscopic A substance that attracts and absorbs water through the air.

melting point The temperature at which a solid material becomes liquid.

metallurgy The science and study of metals and of fabricating things with metal, or metal engineering.

microprinting 3D printing on a very small, microscopic scale. Related to nanoprinting.

microwelding Welding on a small scale, usually involving miniature tools and laser beams. The results can be microscopic. Metals in 3D printing are often sintered using microwelding.

nanoprinting 3D printing on a microscopically small scale. Used for the creation of nanoproducts.

noninvasive imaging systems Test techniques that allow us to look inside things without cutting them open or damaging them. One of the earliest methods of looking inside a human body was through X-rays. Other noninvasive methods include magnetic resonance imaging and ultrasound.

petrochemical A chemical made from fossil fuels, particularly petroleum. Many of these are not biodegradable and do not safely break down into natural elements in the environment.

polylactic acid (PLA) A biodegradable plastic used for many things, including medical tools and equipment, implants, and disposable products.

print bed The base plate on which everything in a 3D printing project is built.

scaffold A structure of semisolid and solid gels and connective tissue used as a frame or skeleton on which to layer bioinks. It provides support and gives shape to bioprint projects.

selective laser sintering (SLS) A method of 3D printing that uses powdered or bead forms of the construction material on a powder bed. A distributing arm spreads a thin layer of powder or beads over any previous layers, and a movable arm aims a laser at the powdered material. The material melts and bonds to any lower layers.

sintering The process of bonding the material used in 3D printing, in particular plastic and metal. Sintering usually requires heat to fuse layers of material. Sintering bonds the layers, creating a single unit.

slicing Using computer software (called a slicer) to convert a 3D CAD design into individual 2D layers. These serve as instructions and blueprints for the 3D printer, which reads the slicer's instructions.

slurry A wet mix of solids and liquids. In pottery, clay and water are stirred into a slurry to decorate turned pots. In manufacturing, paper pulp and water form a slurry that can shaped into packaging material.

stereolithography (SL or SLA) 3D printing using a liquid resin that is cured using ultraviolet lasers to solidify the pattern one layer at a time.

thermoplastic A form of plastic that can be heated and shaped multiple times. The opposite of thermoset plastic, which can be melted and shaped only once.

thermoplastic elastomer (TPE) A mix of plastics and rubbers which are thermoplastic, rather than thermoset, and can be stretched repeatedly.

thermoset A material that can be melted only once, after which it will not be possible to change the form, even with heat. The opposite of thermoplastic.

tissue compatibility Tissue with common antigens so the body won't reject transplanted material.

two-photon lithography A microprinting method using liquid resin and a pair of UV laser beams to solidify and cure the resin into microscopically detailed forms.

veneer A thin layer forming a surface, usually used in reference to older furniture and built-in cabinetry.

vitrify To fuse materials into one glassy mass. High-grade ceramics vitrify together. Porcelain is hard and brittle and thin because it has vitrified.

FURTHER INFORMATION

Instructional Videos

**Additive Manufacturing–
Direct Metal Laser Sintering DMLS Technology**

https://www.youtube.com/watch?v=rEfdO4p4SFc

A well-done video illustrating how DMLS is used in manufacturing.

How It Is Made: 3D Printing Filament

https://www.youtube.com/watch?v=OEkksADFjP8

A commercially made video on how plastic filament is made.

How Metal 3D Printing Works

https://www.youtube.com/watch?v=da5IsmZZ-tw

A professional video on the science and methods of 3D printing using metals.

Maker's Muse

https://www.youtube.com/user/TheMakersMuse

An enthusiast who tests 3D printing techniques, materials, and printers for consumers to help hobbyists.

3D Printing and Metal Casting Jewelry with the Form 2–Prop: 3D

https://www.youtube.com/watch?v=ILzn5ahSoM4

A practical video aimed at hobby makers with a focus on costume and prop creation with prop maker Bill Doran.

3D Printing Nerd

https://www.youtube.com/channel/UC_7aK9PpYTqt08ERh1MewlQ

An enthusiast with many tutorials on 3D printing, examples of successful 3D prints, popular 3D printing trends, and 3D printing projects.

Materials Reference

Materials Used In 3D Printing And Additive Manufacturing

http://www.azom.com/article.aspx?ArticleID=8132

Reference material provided by AZoM, a leading publication of the 3D printing community. There are downloadable copies.

Stratasys: Materials

http://www.stratasys.com/materials

A commercial site with a downloadable reference on 3D-printable plastics.

3D Printing Basics

http://www.3ders.org/3d-printing-basics.html

A starter's reference from a 3D news site.

Online Articles

Fun with Flexible 3D Printing Filaments

http://makezine.com/projects/
make-42/fun-with-flexibles

An article by Matt Stultz for Makezine (a maker community resource) that gives advice on the settings and steps to take when using flexible filament as well as the mistakes to avoid.

Future House: 3-D Printed and Ready to Fly

https://www.nytimes.com/2016/07/21/us/future-house-3-d-printed-and-ready-to-fly.html

An article by Paulette Perhach of the *New York Times* focusing on the production of housing and shelter using 3D printing methods.

Sweet Dimension: 3-D Printed Chocolate

http://today.uconn.edu/2017/04/sweet-dimension-3-d-printed-chocolate

An article by Emily Fitzpatrick of *UConn Today* on a University of Connecticut class project using chocolate in 3D printing.

The 3-D Printing Revolution

https://hbr.org/2015/05/the-3-d-printing-revolution

Richard D'Aveni of the *Harvard Business Review* covers the increasing impact of 3D printing on industrial manufacture and productivity.

Your Next Pair of Shoes Could Come From a 3-D Printer

https://www.nytimes.com/2016/09/15/business/smallbusiness/your-next-pair-of-shoes-could-come-from-a-3-d-printer.html?_r=0

Constance Gutske of the *New York Times* writes on the increasing use of 3D printing in manufacturing.

Websites

History of 3D Printing

https://redshift.autodesk.com/history-of-3d-printing

A timeline of the origins and current trends in 3D printing from a 3D modeling and printing news source supported by Autodesk (a prominent CAD program creator).

Sculpteo/blog

https://www.sculpteo.com/blog

A news and information blog for hobby-level 3D printing makers.

Thingiverse

https://www.thingiverse.com

An online resource for 3D designs. Provides beginners with a wide range of objects they can produce themselves using school or hobby-level 3D printing labs.

3D Printing Industry

http://3dprintingindustry.com/3d-printing-basics-free-beginners-guide

A beginner's guide to 3D printing from a reputable 3D printing news outlet.

3D Printing Materials

https://www.3dhubs.com/materials

An extensive list of 3D printing materials by 3D Hubs, which is a site that can print your 3D models using these materials.

INDEX

Page numbers in **boldface** are illustrations. Entries in **boldface** are glossary terms.

ABOUT THE AUTHOR

Peg Robinson is a writer and editor specializing in researched educational materials and white papers. She graduated from the University of California at Santa Barbara in 2008, with honors, and attended Pacifica Graduate Institution. She served for two years as a docent for Opus Archives, focusing on converting historically significant audio recordings to digital format, securing valuable material in a less fragile recording medium. She lives in Rhode Island, with her daughter and her cat and dog.